To Bear Witness
Revised, Updated and Expanded Edition

To Bear Witness
A Journey of Healing and Solidarity

Kevin M. Cahill, M.D.

Fordham University Press
New York 2013

Fordham University Press has no
responsibility for the persistence
or accuracy of URLs for external
or third-party Internet websites
referred to in this publication
and does not guarantee that any
content on such websites is, or will
remain, accurate or appropriate.

Fordham University Press also
publishes its books in a variety
of electronic formats. Some content
that appears in print may not be
available in electronic books.

Library of Congress
Control Number: 2013935812

Printed in the United States of America
15 14 13   5 4 3 2 1

Second Edition

All royalties from the sale of this book
go to the training of humanitarian workers.

For Kate

Contents

Part Two: Academia *75*

Part Three: Continuity *126*

Part Four: Personal *201*

Acknowledgements

As with the first edition, this volume was designed by my dear friend Massimo Vignelli; design production by Mauro Sarri of Vignelli Associates. It was retyped and carefully reviewed by Jenna Felz, Denis Cahill and Rachel Stein-Holmes. I express my gratitude to Fordham University Press, its Director, Fredrick Nachbaur; to my French editor, Maggie Doyle of Robert Laffont, Paris; to Fordham University President Joseph McShane, S.J.; and to my colleagues and staff at Fordham's Institute of International Humanitarian Affairs (IIHA) www.fordham.edu/iiha
The spirit of my wife Kate can be found throughout these pages, permeating this book as she did every fiber of my being from the time we were teenagers in love, through the decades of shared partnership when we tried, in words as well as deeds, to devote ourselves to a mutual search for human rights and peace with justice.

Introduction

Shortly after my wife died in 2004, the first edition of this book was conceived as an exploration of some of the main activities of our shared lives. I selected articles, essays, book introductions, speeches and op-ed pieces that were originally published, if at all, in journals, magazines and texts, many long out of print; some were more than fifty years old. At first they just elicited memories, but gradually a coherence emerged – motivating purposes that defined our marriage.

On rereading them I discovered an almost eerie relevance to current national debates. In fact, many consider the very essence of our national soul and could, I then suggested, be read as prescient parables for the crises of the twenty-first century. Some essays consider the influences of youth and family, of lasting lessons learned at the kitchen table; others consider university and history, ethnicity and diplomacy, medicine, public health and politics. All were personal, and offered opinions and observations that bore witness to my obligation, as I saw it, as an international physician and humanitarian worker to expose, especially in our privileged nation, the sufferings and inequities experienced by the downtrodden masses of the world.

They were all influenced by the remarkable woman to whom this book, and my life, are dedicated. It was she who encouraged my enthusiasms and commitments, and then gave guidance on the journey, wherever it would lead us. She had very definite opinions on the inalienable rights of all human beings; she was willing to listen carefully to, and then gently influence, arguments at the very heart of foreign affairs and domestic health programs. Her unwavering support helped create the wonderful life we shared – a life of service and joy, of travel and discovery, a life where asylum seekers, dreamers, and failures found refuge in our home, and became family realities, as friends from around the world sought our help.

Nine years have passed since the first edition of this book. It has gone through multiple printings and been translated into French. I have now updated the text by, once again, selecting recent, hopefully, relevant, articles and speeches that reflect the continuity of an on-going journey of healing and solidarity.

Part One: Locations

During the past half century I have undertaken medical and humanitarian missions, or lectured on these topics, in 65 countries in Africa, Asia, Latin America and Europe; my wife Kate was my partner in 45 nations, often under very trying and sometimes dangerous circumstances. This book reflects a peripatetic life, but one where all the travels and works were—and, for me, continue to be—based on an awareness of our good fortune, and resultant responsibilities.

I have selected four geographic areas for this section. Each of the short chapters tells a tale of both healing, for that is the ultimate goal of a physician's efforts, and of solidarity, for that becomes a necessity in crisis zones if one is to grow beyond the traditional privileges of the doctor-patient relationship and emerge with any sense of decency and dignity. The essays hopefully also indicate the metamorphosis that occurred in my own life as I became immersed in the tragedies of third world countries. Those poor and sick populations, surviving incredible challenges, became my teachers, my role models in how to live with courage and joy in a harsh but still hopeful world.

We lived for several wonderful years in the early 1960s in the Middle East. In those Vietnam War years, all physicians were drafted into military service. After graduating from medical school and training in New York, the U.S. Navy allowed me to spend a year completing a graduate degree in tropical medicine in England. I was then assigned to a research unit in Cairo, Egypt as Director of Epidemiology and Chief of Clinical Tropical Medicine, rather wonderful positions for a young doctor free to study major epidemics all over the Middle East and Africa.

This photo shows me in my Navy uniform on a border where the Kurds were fleeing from Iraq into Turkey – a phenomenon

that was a regular occurrence in those years, and is still a fact of life today in the area. The refugees were spreading a parasitic disease, cutaneous leishmaniasis, across southeast Turkey. I established a base in Diyarbakir, one of the few walled cities that withstood the onslaught of Genghis Khan. Our task was to identify the causative agent and try to contain the epidemic. I spent six weeks on horseback, protected by some fifty Turkish cavalrymen, on the steppes of the Tigris-Euphrates valley. We rode through historic hill towns—Urfa, Siirt, and around the shores of Lake Van—eating over open fires and sleeping in the shadows of monuments in the home of civilization. We were able to localize and eradicate the epidemic.

The Middle East

One year after caring for Pope John Paul II, following the assassination attempt that almost ended his life in 1981, he asked that I travel to war-torn Lebanon as his personal representative. I tried to capture in this article the individual trauma and determination I experienced there—and that is still evident in the streets of Beirut more than thirty years later. The op-ed piece elicited many, some quite hostile, letters.

The article about Libya was chosen by a foreign policy association as one of the best journalistic pieces of that particular year. It raises questions concerning honesty and integrity that are as valid today as when I wrote this essay.

The article on Gaza again reflects the unusual opportunity that a physician has in a war zone; one can have rapid access to scenes of great trauma, work with professional colleagues in hospitals and casualty centers, and then report on the human costs of conflicts. I undertook this journey as the Chief Advisor on Humanitarian and Public Health Issues for the President of the United Nations General Assembly; the report was selected by the United Nations that year as the essay distributed on World Humanitarian Day, August 19th.

Beirut's Smell of Death
The New York Times, 1982

Armenian scholars no longer search for God in the Near East School of Theology in West Beirut. The cool archives room in the cellar is now a blood bank, and the conference hall where ecclesiastical nuances were once the topic of discussion now contains two operating tables for assembly line amputations and a bin for severed limbs.

This month the Palestinian Red Crescent Society incorporated the School of Theology into one of the most remarkable healthcare delivery services in the world, one that maintains twenty five dispensaries and a two thousand bed hospital system serving a half million people still surviving the air and ground attacks that threaten the existence of West Beirut. The world famous American University of Beirut Hospital is the backup center for the field hospital at the theology school, and I had the privilege of examining patients and consulting with doctors in both places last week. Medicine is that rare discipline that permits almost instant acceptability by all sides in a conflict. It offers a unique perspective on war, as close as one gets to the viewpoint of the victim.

I undertook a tour of the war ravaged areas of Lebanon at the request of the Pontifical Mission, and I worked in that scarred and tortured land once fabled for its beauty. Square blocks of the ancient biblical cities of Tyre and Sidon have been bombed away. We could not find a single intact structure – nor a single person – in the formally Christian town of Damur, and Israeli bulldozers were wiping away evidence that Palestinian camps, once home for tens of thousands of families, even existed.

Statistics are a game that politicians play in war. People far from the scene are having a great debate in the American press about the accuracy of death figures in Lebanon. But there is nothing subtle about the current carnage in Beirut if one can recognize blood, or smell a festering wound, or feel the feverish head of a dying child. There is no mystery about the scope of this tragedy, if one walks the wards of the university hospital of the School of Theology and sees the limbless bodies, the fractured faces, the blind, the burned. These are real people, men and women and children, hundreds of them, and no amount of sophistry can dehumanize the horrors of this war into a sterile column of figures. They were not numbers I examined; they were the innocent civilian debris of a war not of their making but caused by policies that have left them a stateless people. Now they have their dead and their maimed to nourish their hatred and determination.

We saw young refugees in Tripoli in the far north of Lebanon who had traveled hundreds of miles over mountains only to find that their parents were lost somewhere on the trek. The frightened, almost hopeless stare of a hungry orphan can tell a great deal about the wisdom of war. I met an Austrian woman whose husband and two children were gone when she returned home from her job as a nurse in West Beirut. They lived in a camp that had been destroyed by incendiary and cluster bombs. "I could find no one," she said, "only bits and pieces of arms and legs. We just pushed the whole camp into a hole and covered it with plastic and earth." Wherever we traveled, official statistics released by the occupying forces referred only to Lebanese casualties, so one often heard ludicrously low estimates. It was as if the Palestinians—those hundreds of thousands of women and children who had nothing to do with the Palestinian Liberation Organization fighters—simply did not exist.

Aid is received by the governing authorities only for displaced Lebanese who, to be sure, deserve international help, for they have suffered inordinately since the civil war broke out in 1975. The occupying forces refuse, however, to accept any direct assistance for Palestinians, stopping even food and medicines from being taken to the ravaged, rat infested ghettos of West Beirut.

Unless the indiscriminate bombing and shelling cease for good, the load of shattered limbs discarded from the Near East School of Theology will grow. While the wise men struggle slowly with the semantics of peace, panic stricken victims scream psychotically in halls where scholars once pondered the words of God. Hatred abounds, and the legacy of bitterness that will be reflected a generation hence in cripples on the streets of Beirut will pose a greater threat to the security of the area than militaristic minds seem capable of considering now.

The painful process toward reconciliation and eventual peace may be best symbolized today in the joint efforts at healing by Armenians, Palestinians, Christian, and Moslem Lebanese, Norwegian volunteers, and this American who shall long remember the privilege of making clinical rounds in the Near East School of Theology. Examining patients while shells exploded and fires raged nearby, and with the sick smell of death and disease overwhelming my senses, I wondered what ends could ever justify these means.

A Doctor's Reflections on the Libyan Situation
America, 1986

American planes were bombing Libya last week as I was returning from a medical mission to Yemen. For a quarter of a century I have had the privilege of working part of each year in the "developing" lands of Africa, Latin America, and the Mideast, serving as a physician during epidemics and in refugee camps, amid the chaos of natural disasters ranging from floods and droughts to earthquakes and famines. My view of these lands, with the smells, sounds and feelings of naked, exposed human beings, must be the opposite of the bombardier seeing that reality, through missile sights, as faceless targets and goals.

Having seen twenty-five years ago how the greatness and beauty of America were distorted abroad when presented solely through military and commercial ventures, I proposed we take advantage of the understanding and goodwill that flow from shared humane endeavors. I discovered, in the Middle East of the early 1960s, that even when there were few areas for agreement, it was still possible to focus on common convictions – that mothers and babies, for example, should be nourished and housed.

On those unfilled and basic needs, bridges can be built as a mutually beneficial alternative to endless recriminations and threats. These ideas took root and flourished for a period among internationalists in the United States but seem now to be fading fast in the afterglow of neoisolationism that sees America's destiny more in terms of East-West conflict than North-South accommodation.

Once again, we are beginning to convince ourselves that we

have the right to dictate to other nations rather than win their support by sharing, or at least understanding, their problems. Once again, we apparently see no wrong in arrogating for ourselves the self-anointed roles of international judge and enforcer. History does not indicate that we will be treated kindly. The worldwide acclaim Israelis won when they captured Adolf Eichmann, convicted him in a court of law, and executed him for crimes against humanity can be contrasted with the loss of esteem and the international condemnation that followed the indiscriminate bombing of Beirut and the Sabra and Shatila refugee camp slaughters. No matter how frustrated a major nation becomes, it cannot take revenge on innocent people without paying a terrible price. That is the failed policy of the jungle, and it destroys the integrity and legitimacy of a nation at home and abroad. We condemn terrorism against our civilians, but those we kill in revenge are just as dead as the American victims and, it turns out, usually just as innocent.

In reflecting on America's response, I do not justify Libyan – or any other – violations of our inherent right to live in safety and without fear. But we will not secure that by abandoning the rich traditions and principles that are the essence of America. We cannot let truth become the victim of expediency without even a comment. It was appalling to arrive home and realize how minimal were the editorial questions raised about the Libyan exercise, for it was almost as if it would be anti-American to voice concern in the middle of a patriotic orgy. When the President declared that he had never intended to kill Muammar el-Qaddafi – or even overthrow him – it was surprising that not a single newspaper or TV commentator in my orbit asked why bombs fell on his home repeatedly, killing his daughter and wounding his sons. Truth is an essential quality for credibility with our allies, and discussion and dissent are necessary in a free society.

To maintain the civilization we enjoy, we cannot resolve differences by disregarding international law. We are obsessed with our own anger but seem incapable of appreciating the validity of others' hostility. We do no service to the search for peace by labeling our opponents "mad" or "terrorists." Terrorism will continue to be a method in conflicts though the

Middle East as long as the Palestinian problem remains an open wound. Generations have survived in refugee camps in that area because of political decisions beyond Palestinian control, and terrorism will flow from that bitter well, with or without Libyan Colonel Qaddafi. Guerrilla tactics have always been the recourse of the underdog when competing with superior opponents, and we shall not change that approach by retaliation alone. The simplistic solutions of a Rambo – even if applauded for the moment by an emotional public – will ultimately fail. The tide of history is against those who believe that military might can prevail. Only the hand of healing will bind the wounds of mistrust and division that prolong our suffering.

Gaza – Destruction and Hope
A United Nations Report, 2009

My professional career in international health and humanitarian relief has, over the last 50 years, taken me to numerous disaster areas. I have often known the danger of being caught behind the lines in civil wars, and have shared in the pain and squalor that is the constant fate of those who survive. These experiences have provided a perspective on life – and on man's inhumanity to man – that has been largely fashioned in the crucible of conflicts and refugee camps.

Part of the obligation of those privileged to work in humanitarian assistance is to report on the sufferings of those we serve. We become the voice of the vulnerable, describing as clearly as we can the realities faced by the dispossessed and the helpless. But we do not focus merely on existing evils; we also search for rays of hope in situations where others see only utter despair. There are occasions where our unique experiences and insights can provide foundations for lasting peace. Certainly our suggestions are no less valid than political or diplomatic pronouncements made far from the fray. One way or the other, silence is simply not an option for us. I offer in this report from Gaza both an assessment of the current devastation, and a possible basis for progress.

Seeing Gaza shortly after the Israeli forces departed, in January 2009, after a "total war" invasion reminded me of Dore's 19th

Century engravings of Hell for Dante's *Inferno*. The level of destruction conjured up images of Dresden or Hiroshima at the end of World War II. There were areas in the northern Gaza Strip where not a single structure was standing. An Amnesty International report decried this "wanton destruction" of civilian buildings on a massive scale.

Gaza, a narrow strip of land, 25 miles long by 3 to 7 miles wide, with a population estimated at over 1.4 million, is one of the most densely crowded areas in the world. Its borders, completely surrounded by an Israeli barricade by land, and by its navy on the seacoast, prevent any escape. When war came, there was literally nowhere to flee, no safe haven as neighboring countries are required to provide under international refugee law. The population of Gaza has existed under a hostile occupation for over four decades, and in recent years there has been a steady reduction of all imports and exports, slowly strangling the private economy, leading towards the highest unemployment rates, and among the poorest nutrition levels, in the developing world.

Military controls are imposed with a grinding force and overt disdain that is clearly intended to crush the human dignity of a still proud people. The daily humiliations – at border crossings, during constant incursions by soldiers working under ever-changing rules and mandates, the herding of people, like cattle, into barbed wire waiting pens, are all a consistent and pervasive pattern of the occupation.

Israel's "Operation Cast Lead," begun by a bombing campaign on December 27, 2008 and lasting until January 19, 2009, damaged sixteen of Gaza's twenty-seven hospitals and selectively attacked and burned ambulances and many clinics. Thirteen health workers were killed during the three-week assault. The main United Nations warehouses, with all medical and humanitarian supplies, were totally destroyed, and fifteen United Nations schools were severely damaged.

The invasion, according to the World Health Organization, left 1,380 Palestinians dead and 5,380 injured; of the dead, 446 were children, 111 women and 108 elderly. Even higher proportions of women and children were among those seriously wounded. The vast majority of injured were in Gaza City and at the north end of the strip. During the same period, Israel listed fourteen deaths on its side; three were civilians, victims of the Hamas rocket attacks, but most had been accidentally shot by their own forces. These are not the data of a war, but of one-sided slaughter.

Statistics can offer a somewhat cold assessment of the damage inflicted by war. The number of dead can be measured with reasonable accuracy, though some innocent victims are never found, or are buried with understandable disregard for those who caused such grief. The number of wounded is a much more fluid figure. How does one measure pain, or the permanent deformity caused by white phosphorous, or the life-long impact of lost limbs? Do we have any way to calculate the terror from bombings, or from the eerie phosphorous glow that cannot be extinguished, from the resultant burns, or from the scars of panic, and of families broken apart by useless death?

The semantics of war usually disguise obvious truths. Consider phrases such as "friendly fire," "disproportionate response," "collateral damage"; or what does it mean to be the "victor" in a unilateral massacre; or what happens to the soul of a nation when the majority of its 18- and 19-year-olds, both male and female, fulfilling their army obligation, casually carry M16 machine guns in public malls and streets, learning early in life how to intimidate their neighbors?

The entire commercial zone of Gaza and other industrial plants, including ice cream and biscuit factories, along with the territory's only asphalt plant and 22 of the 29 cement factories, were systematically demolished as the Israeli army withdrew, clearly demonstrating the intent of crushing a community by collective punishment. Even the withdrawal was timed with a cynical disregard for world opinion. Israel had begun the assault with the tacit approval of the United States in the dying days of the cooperative Bush administration. They brought back their troops the day before President Obama's inauguration in order not to tarnish his image with a sordid conflict in a volatile region. But on the ground there was no escaping the fact that this was a war using American weapons of incredible power and precision guided missiles against the home made rockets, gasoline bombs and rocks that are the major weapons of long oppressed peoples.

All the schools were closed the day I arrived because heavy

rains had left a majority of the children without any dry clothes. Emergency tents had either leaked so badly or completely collapsed into the flowing mud quagmire that was now home for over 200,000 people displaced when their houses were destroyed. The water and sanitation systems were also severely damaged, and sewage flooded down open streets and gutters into the sea.

The United Nations Relief Works Agency (UNRWA) and the Palestinian Authority had made funds available for emergency rentals, but there were few apartments available. Reconstruction cannot begin because Israel does not permit the importation of steel, cement or glass, among other building materials. They also restricted the importation of lentils, pasta, tomato paste and juice by some incomprehensible logic that these items may pose a security threat. In a particularly cruel twist, batteries for hearing aids used by deaf children cannot be imported, condemning these unfortunates to a world of silence. Despite these Draconian regulations, UNRWA has been able to provide a basic food supply to over a million refugees in the Gaza Strip. I visited a food station where hundreds of displaced persons waited to collect their meager staples of rice, sugar, lentils and cooking oil. While this program may save people from starvation, it is a diet that does not prevent the highest level of anemia in the region, with alarming rates of childhood stunting due to inadequate nutrition.

I made clinical rounds in the partially destroyed Palestinian Red Crescent Society Hospital (the Palestinian Red Crescent is a full partner in the International Federation of the Red Cross and Red Crescent Societies, to which the American Red Cross and Israel's Magen David Adom also belong). One night, during the height of the campaign, doctors were forced to evacuate hundreds of patients after an incendiary bomb caused a fire that consumed the top four floors of the institution. Imagine trying to move a full intensive care unit and neonatal patients on respirators and incubators, wheeling critically ill patients down debris laden streets, manually pumping breathing machines, until they could deposit their terrified charges in another hospital.

Another surgeon told of operating on a wounded man while bombs dropped on the hospital; I later examined that patient's massive soft tissue damage and fractured femur treated by external fixation. The doctor also described injured patients with grossly infected wounds because they had not been able to be evacuated from their homes for up to seven days after being injured. Besides these obvious war injuries, other medical crises loom. Forty percent of those with chronic diseases, such as hypertension or diabetes, were denied routine drugs for the full duration of the invasion. Deafness due to sonic booms and bombs, mental health problems due to trauma, loss of loved ones or being forced to live in utterly changed circumstances (in tents or amid the rubble), are other major medical problems.

The gross disparity in the number of victims suffered by the two sides, along with the graphic media images of senseless destruction, may, it seems to me, actually offer an opportunity. The fundamental evils of continued forced isolation and economic strangulation have finally come to the fore. American Congressmen visiting Gaza have been unable to hide their shock at the levels of destruction. They are fully aware of the central role that the Palestine crisis plays in the broader Arab unrest in the region.

Unless border crossings are promptly, and fully, opened, and supplies for humanitarian aid and reconstruction, as well as commercial goods for the private sector, are allowed to flow in an uninterrupted stream, the suffering will inevitably accelerate. Unless the destroyed water and sewer systems are quickly repaired, predictable epidemic diseases will occur, claiming more innocent lives. Unless the private sector can rebuild, and get the material resources it needs, the staggering levels of unemployment will continue. Empty rhetoric is a cheap substitute for obviously needed relief and assistance. It is time for the United States of America to demand a halt to Israeli policies and actions that are damaging American interests throughout the Middle East, as well as in Islamic countries around the world.

After leaving Gaza, I traveled to the Israeli town of Sderot, which has been one of the places that has recorded indiscriminate Hamas rocket attacks. There was no evidence of serious structural damage in the town, though concern is evident in the bomb shelters built next to most bus stops and malls. An elaborate alarm system warns the public of incoming rockets.

There are, not incidentally, no preventive alarm systems, or bunkers in Gaza. Palestinians must take refuge in public buildings, and when UNRWA schools were hit during the Gaza invasion, many people were killed and wounded.

In 1982, I was in Beirut on a Vatican mission during a prolonged Israel-Palestine conflict. I wrote an op-ed article for the New York Times that dealt with the clinical horrors of war, the death of innocents – and innocence. The article suggested that unbridled assaults on civilians are very likely to be counter-productive, prompting a radical response from those who had lost loved ones, and whose only recourse was to embrace the traditional weapons of rebels. The article, detailing offenses against helpless women and children, questioned, "What ends could ever justify these means." The op-ed was published just before the very predictable massacres that took place at the Sabra and Shatila camps where over 900 women and children were sacrificed on an alter of folly. Now, over thirty years later, one could insert the word Gaza for Beirut, and tragically, republish the article as current news.

We cannot afford to repeat the past, pursuing a path that offers no hope of peace. Sometimes history suggests that a new administration, with fresh insight, and the necessary political will, can make a courageous change. When General Charles de Gaulle was elected President of France in 1958, it was with the vigorous support of the military. Shortly after taking office he reviewed the Algerian quagmire, where torture and repression were staining the essence of his beloved France. He concluded that his nation should offer Algerians full independence. De Gaulle survived an assassination attempt, and an attempted military coup, but France emerged free from a sordid colonial oppression.

A more recent historical example is the realization of peace in Northern Ireland. There, neighbors divided by religion and culture had endured decades of killings and maimings. Peace came through dialogue, not by dictating a resolution, but by finding common ground among all parties. Two years ago, the then Irish Prime Minister, Bertie Ahern, told a Council on Foreign Relations audience in New York that the mediators communicated with "the bad guys" as well as with "the establishment." During the question period, a member of the audience, citing the Middle East, noted, "We cannot talk with Hezbollah or Hamas for they have been labeled 'terrorist organizations' for fighting with Israel." The Prime Minister responded – simply but bluntly – "then you will never find peace." That lesson is obvious today in Gaza. It seems impossible that peace will ever be found there without involving the democratically elected Hamas government. As in Northern Ireland, an inclusive process is the only way forward.

If President Obama, in reviewing the longstanding Arab-Israel conflict, were to withdraw support for the failed policies of the past against the Palestinian people, and truly foster a peace process, then, when a new Israeli government is formed, it might well, willingly, search for a new path toward peace, one that is consistent with the nobility of a people this nation has long admired and assisted.

By the time refugee crises had become an almost regular part of Somali life in the 1980s, I had already worked in that country for part of every year for almost two decades. I had walked the length of the country, studying the diseases of nomads, from the Ethiopian border in the extreme North, across the desert and scrub lands of the Horn of Africa, and down through the lush riverine banana plantations to the southern swamps of central Africa. As one of the very few physicians to return with regularity, I was asked to direct a massive and complex humanitarian emergency relief operation. The nation, with few doctors, was overwhelmed. What was surprising was how much one had to devise on the spot—developing, with few precedents and

even fewer accepted standards — life saving programs on a vast scale, establishing food and shelter services for hundreds of thousands of poor, sick, frightened people. I tried to create order out of chaos, becoming involved, for the first time in my medical life, in issues that ranged from the construction of huts to assuring adequate sanitation, water supplies, security, and even an efficient system for the disposal of the dead. This had to be done in keeping, as far as possible, with local customs and traditions. My wife would often share time with me in these refugee camps, giving critical support and putting a warm, human face to often harsh realities. Ours was a marriage made in heaven, and honed to perfection in some of the hell holes on earth.

Somalia

These articles reflect a forty-plus year love affair with the people and land of a now "failed state." I was present at the birth of the Somali Republic, a birth of joy and hope and promise. Thirty years later, I was also present when the government of Somalia imploded, a death of a nation caused by corruption, incompetence, and international politics. In 2011 I returned to the bombed out shell of Mogadishu with the President of the General Assembly and Secretary General of the United Nations, viewing the destructive results of twenty years of lawlessness. My technical papers documenting medical and epidemiological studies were once collected in a small textbook, Health on the Horn of Africa, *a volume I was once told had "one of the lowest sales records in publishing history," and in a later book,* Somalia: A Perspective.

For a U.S. Role in Somalia
The New York Times, 1977

All around Brava, except to the east, the red sands swirl. Sparse scrub bush and the thorny acacia tree somehow survive in the parched earth. This is the land Ahmed Mohamed knew for forty years as he herded camels and goats across the semi-desert of Somaliland in an endless quest for water.

This was the traditional land of the nomads of East Africa, and it sustained a society and a culture that could trace roots to ancient Egypt. This was the Land of Punt where incense trees grew wild, and epic poems told tales of overcoming hardships, and of periodic decimating diseases. It is predominantly a harsh and arid area isolated from its neighbors by forbidding semi desert.

But in 1975, that world ended as the Sahelian drought moved eastward across Africa, destroying herds and scorching all plant life. The last stop on the trek of the drought victims was the shore of the Indian Ocean. For Somalia, on the Horn of Africa, was the end of the line. There was nowhere left to flee and two hundred seventy thousand nomads sought the remnants of their lives in refugee camps. Thirty-one thousand died of starvation and infection.

There was another facet to the tragedy: the challenge of resettling a whole population who knew only the care of animals that were now gone. They had to be molded into an utterly new, more stable way of life by a nation with few resources and even fewer options. The alternative to such drastic redirection was death. To the east of Brava was the hope of the future – the sea, the untapped resource of the Indian Ocean.

How can a nation of nomads be made into fisherman? How does one change an age-old disdain for the slimy creatures of the deep and make an entire society recognize the dignity as well as the nutritional value of the sea? There are many similarities between the desert and the sea: the isolation, the silence, the flow of wave or dune, the dependence on wind and star, sun and rain, and, in particular, the necessity for that peculiar courage and wisdom of the lonely striving against the elements. Somalia has begun forging fishermen out of nomads.

The Soviet Union transported 140,000 people and their meager belongings to four agricultural and three fishing camps. Most of the nomads had never seen the sea, much less knew how to swim, or man a boat, or care for the trim and tackle of a fisherman. Yet today, two years after beginning this experiment in national transformation, the former nomads are bringing in 600,000 pounds of fish per day, live in fixed communities with schools and hospitals, with canning factories and export quotas. They are a people with new dreams as well as new realities.

Somalia is much in the news as East and West contend for the future of the Indian Ocean. The strategic significance of Somalia's vast coastline, from which the oil-shipping lanes at the entrance to the Red Sea and the southern end of the Suez Canal can be blocked, has long attracted the attention of the superpowers.

When the United States discontinued aid to Somalia in 1969 on the dubious premise that the Somali "flag of convenience" was flown by foreign companies trading with North Vietnam, the poor but proud young nation sought an increasing percentage of its critical help from the Soviet Union. Gradually a Soviet presence permeated the Horn. That pervasive influence, however, became offensive when the Russians offered military help last year to Somalia's arch-enemy, Ethiopia.

Selfishly, the Somalis now see America's presence as a balance to the overwhelming force of the Russians, but they also hope that the United States might recognize an overdue opportunity to correct the unnecessary slights that have characterized our past relations. Somalia asks if we will help resettle destitute nomads, join in the adventure of changing Ahmed Mohamed from a herdsman to a fisherman, share in creating a new agricultural revolution, and contribute to the development of permanent homes and schools for the nomads.

There is precious little time for decision; the Horn is explosive, and the options are clear.

Palm Sunday in Somalia
Catholic New York, 1981

When the Nazarene entered Jerusalem astride a donkey and the crowds placed palms before His feet, a ceremony of welcome was begun that has been renewed annually for almost two thousand years. The Gospels tell us of the many varied faces that came together in those narrow tropical streets to see the Messiah—dark Africans, those from Galilee and Cyrene, slaves and aristocrats from all sectors of the Roman Empire.

It may be difficult to recapture the vibrancy of that scene when, well nourished and well dressed, we hear the Passion recounted through a microphone and gather our palms at the rear of a church before joining neighbors for a walk in the comfort and security of America. Somehow we seem to have lost the poetry that comes with the cacophony of sounds that are part of the tropics. One might think that the earthy smells and the hot, moist climate would crush the joy and spirit of Palm Sunday, but two weeks ago in Somalia, I found a vitality, sincerity, and beauty that we in America would do well to emulate.

I attended Palm Sunday services in the old Italian Cathedral in the capital city of Mogadishu. Its twin stone towers are the tallest points in that ancient Islamic port on the Indian Ocean; the towers have become landmarks for relief workers who are coming in ever-growing numbers to help the largest refugee population in the world today. Volunteers from all over the world have begun to open their hearts and give assistance to an almost forgotten people in an utterly neglected part of Africa.

I have had the privilege of making annual medical research trips in Somalia for many years. When I was last there a year and a half ago, there were a half million refugees gathered in makeshift camps. Over 90 percent were women and children, and the smell of death was pervasive. There was virtually no foreign assistance, with only three medical volunteers in the entire country.

Today the onslaught continues. Over 3,000 new refugees arrive daily, and the total camp population now exceeds 1,300,000. Famine, drought, and epidemic disease take their toll, but the number of refugees still steadily increases. The world is now beginning to respond with hundreds of volunteers sharing in the crisis, and charitable agencies from Europe and America are providing food and medicine in many camps.

This year on Palm Sunday, Somali Catholics were joined in their procession around the cathedral by followers of Christ from many lands—men and women who had come to serve the refugees. There were Indian and Asian workers, young Swedish and American volunteers, mixed with the Italian and English residents who had stayed to bridge the gap between colonial and modern independent Africa.

Despite stultifying heat the bishop was in full regalia, for this was a celebration initiating Holy Week. The white cassocks of friars, nuns, and altar boys blended well with the casual, cool garb of the sweating congregation. But neither insects nor weather could suppress the spirit, and there was an almost palpable sense of common involvement that reminded me of the spirit that must have pervaded the palm-lined streets of Jerusalem so long ago.

Starving Refugees Overwhelm Somalia
The New York Times, 1982

In Somalia, the world's largest refugee population lives with the specter of famine and death. Death may be very gentle after all. An Irish physician-poet once observed how often the final act of life evades rash adults, "those arrogant knights who fling themselves against him in their fights;" but, he noted, "to the loveliest he loves to call, and he has with him those whose ways were mild and beautiful, and many a little child."

The call of death is common today along the Ogaden-Somali border, and children are summoned most often. By seeing the starved skeletal frames of the young and realizing the overwhelming burden of poverty, illness, and violence that war has had on the world's largest refugee population, even the physician can appreciate death as a gentle release from suffering.

According to the United Nations High Commissioner for Refugees (UNHCR), there are now more refugees in Africa than in Southeast Asia, and Somalia bears the largest burden. There are more refugees in Somali camps than in all the Cambodian and Vietnamese camps combined. But few in our nation are even aware of the Somali problem, and fewer still know that the number of refugees and the severity of their plight exceeds the Cambodian catastrophe. Africa is, in fact, being penalized for generously accepting refugees; somehow, the obscene practice of repelling refugees in Southeast Asia has touched the American spirit.

The amount of American aid committed to alleviate the current tragedy of Cambodian refugees is many times greater than that even being considered by our government for all of Africa. Since the United States is the largest donor to UNHCR, our priorities have also influenced international perspective; the 1980 budget of UNHCR allocates almost three times more funds to Southeast Asia than it does to Africa, despite the glaring fact that there are far more refugees in Africa. The United States' response to the Somali plight has, to date, been quite restrained. Our failure to help substantially is probably not intentional neglect, but rather a reflection of our ignorance of Somalia in particular, and of Africa in general. The American media must be stimulated to consider the African refugee scene and respond in a manner appropriate to our heritage and ability. We cannot, as Pope John Paul II reminded us at Yankee Stadium, "give merely the crumbs of our table to Lazarus at the door; we must learn to give of our substance and not merely our abundance."

For many decades I have worked annually among the Somalis, trekking with the nomads for weeks on end while tracing their diseases. They are tough and proud people, who eke out an existence by herding camels and goats over a lunar like landscape. Survival in such an area, where daily temperatures often exceed 100 degrees Fahrenheit and life is an endless search for water, requires a philosophical approach. The people have learned to endure drought, and they expect periodic famine.

Five years ago, when the great Sahelian drought moved eastward over Africa to terminate in Somalia, I also worked in their relief camps. At that time, families who had known only the migratory life of the herder were recycled for settlement on arable land or along the vast Horn of Africa's Indian Ocean coastline. In one of the most remarkable and successful national experiments in modern times, nomads were transformed into farmers and fishermen.

Today, Somalia is in the throes of a far greater crisis. It has a refugee problem without parallel in modern times, caused by a vast influx of starving women and children from the war-torn Ogaden area. Somalia has quietly and steadily accepted the refugees of the Ogaden, for the majority are ethnic brothers and sisters who speak the same language and share religious and cultural bonds. Nevertheless this admirable and fraternal national feeling is reaching the breaking point, since there are now over one million refugees in a total population of five million.

Furthermore, women and children account for 90 percent of the most dependent refugees, those requiring daily feeding and housing in camps. The men in these families are gone; some have been killed in the Ogaden war, many in bombing and strafing raids that have characterized Cuba's and Russia's contribution to the overt Ethiopian effort at permanently depopulating the contested area; other men continue to fight in one of the Somali Liberation Front units; while a few remain in the bush with their dying livestock.

Late last year, the Somali government asked me to conduct an urgent review of its refugee problems. During my stay, I made medical rounds in emergency camps on the embattled frontier and deep in the interior. In a typical camp, a single young Somali doctor labored to serve up to fifty thousand sick, frightened, homeless people. He worked with almost no laboratory or surgical equipment, few nurses, and grossly inadequate drugs and medical supplies in a "hospital" or clinic made of thatch and mud.

The camps that the nomad women have constructed from mud and thatch are infested with disease-carrying insects. None of the camps I visited had latrines; the only water supply is in the parched beds of neighboring rivers or stagnant wells that serve animals as well as humans.

I visited transit camps near the border, where new arrivals are screened, and three of the large "permanent" settlements where survivors are sent to attempt a life of some self-reliance by initiating modest farming projects, such as growing corn and papayas. I revisited hospitals in Mogadishu and Hargeisa to see the general health service of Somalia begin to collapse. Even now, I cannot eradicate the image and smell of a bullet-shattered limb on a woman who had to be carried by camel over 70 miles to the safety of the border before any medical attention could be provided; I cannot forget vacant stares and the bloated bellies of babies dying from starvation by the dozens.

Infectious disease of almost every variety is rife—malaria, tuberculosis, hepatitis, dysentery, bronchitis. The potential for a truly decimating epidemic, of cholera for example, is frighteningly predictable. The death rate is astronomic; one camp of 41,000 women and children had 2,000 deaths in two weeks, with 41 pregnant women dying from dysentery during the week I visited the camp.

To put that latter figure in perspective, it might be noted that in all of New York State only 28 pregnant women died from any cause last year, and not one resulted from infection. As the Minister for Refugee Affairs, Maj. Gen. Jama Ghaleb phrased the situation: "It is a nightmare that threatens the entire land, and our own resources and present foreign assistance are totally inadequate."

Today, Africa looks to see if America will bar the gate or be brethren to a vast horde of homeless, displaced persons who have no hold on our conscience as do the Vietnamese and Cambodians, except for the overriding fact that they are human and starving. Is it too much to hope, for example, that at least the Black Caucus in Congress might agitate for greater awareness of the problems of Africa? Is it not right to ask that the media help to educate the American public by stressing the scope of the Somali disaster?

Time is rapidly running out on Somalia. Since that nation can no longer cope alone with the largest refugee population in the world today, the specter of massive famine and death falls on all of us in the human family.

A Somali Postscript
A Framework for Survival, 1993

Three months after beginning to edit *A Framework for Survival*, I was working in a Somali refugee camp when American military forces landed on the strobe lit, camera crowded beaches of Mogadishu. That there are radically different approaches to resolving conflicts could not have been more apparent. I thought back to a conference room in New York where we had so recently struggled to blend legal, moral, political, and logistical concerns on health, human rights, and humanitarian assistance into a new and creative force in foreign affairs.

Those earlier deliberations seemed especially relevant and timely, reflecting a physician's profound mistrust of "quick fix" therapy, of the dangers in deceiving ourselves that dramatic displays can ever substitute for the tedious tasks required to truly rehabilitate a gravely wounded nation. Changing a humanitarian effort into a security action may offer a temporary respite from the pain of frustration, but it reflects an approach that, while gratifying the short term needs of the healer, fails to resolve the problems of the patient. In fact, the vast scope of military action adversely alters the critical relationship between donor and recipient, drains the finite resources available, and imposes a transient mirage of well-being that simply cannot be sustained.

The Somali story is a sordid one, a shameful tale of selfish global politics gone awry, of superpowers using and then abandoning a client state, of a world silently watching as a corrupt regime annihilated its own population, and a once proud nation slipped into anarchy, with vast death and destruction in its wake.

Somalia offers an almost perfect parable; if there are no easy answers in Somalia at this time there surely are many legitimate questions—hard, demanding ones that are posed in every chapter of *A Framework for Survival*. How these questions are resolved in Somalia may well define future international law, the role of the United Nations, and the relationships of rich and poor nations.

Television and newspaper coverage of the military exercises created an impression of great victories over petty warlords and teenage thugs. No one seemed to ask why the situation had become so desperate before we finally responded, or what was to determine the end point of our visit. No one seemed to question the wisdom of a massive military response, or balance the costs of such an operation with the stated goals. Were 35,400 troops really necessary, and for how long would they remain? Would they merely secure the ports and food convoys, or did they intend to disarm a nomad population and impose a new government? It is conservatively estimated that the military expenses for the first two months will be many times greater than the entire international budget of the last three years for all humanitarian efforts combined.

As I write this, European nations—with minimal risks and maximum media rewards—are competing to have their own troops participate, and enormous financial donations are being sought to underwrite the military costs. But relatively little of this money will go to reconstruct Somalia. Who will bear the costs of restoring the country's civil infrastructure, of reestablishing a functioning society that needs everything from education to police, from housing to a court system, not to mention such essentials as food, crops, tools, and animals? Can we afford merely to indulge in self-gratifying relief operations without realizing that, if there is to be an end to dependence, we must provide opportunities for the Somalis to help themselves? Why not, for instance, create a Somali police force, and allow them to govern and decide who should be disarmed and how?

The relationship between the United States and the United Nations in the Somali military exercise contains the seeds of future disaster. Has the Security Council become a rubber stamp in an era when only one world power remains? Is it in the best, long-term interest of the UN to so unbalance its activities in favor of military exercises? What are the norms that the world will use in deciding where, when, and how to intervene? The current level of hunger and oppression in the southern Sudan, for example, may well be more extensive than the Somali disaster, but the television images of starving infants in Baidoa have made one a genuine humanitarian crisis, while ignorance and inattention leave an impression that the other does not exist.

We must learn to ask the right questions if we are ever to find adequate answers. Somalia's tragedy may be a seminal one, and demands responses that are more complex and more difficult than an inappropriately vast and costly spectacle of American military might. The world clearly needs a better approach. *A Framework For Survival* poses many of the right questions for those who must try, each in his or her own way, to devise a blueprint for the future, one that will be built on the terrible realities of a Somali refugee camp as well as the valid concerns of diplomats in a conference hall.

Shortly after a midnight earthquake destroyed the center of the capital city of Nicaragua, I received a call from their government asking me to establish a health service amidst the ruins. I left New York on a private plane at two in the morning and arrived at the damaged Managua airport while the ground was still shaking and the sky was illuminated with burning buildings. One of the more bizarre aspects of the arrival was to be greeted in the VIP lounge by the American ambassador who introduced me to the pathologically reclusive Howard Hughes. The great aviator, industrialist, and movie maker was well along on his downward spiral and, disheveled, was fleeing his blackened out top floor rooms at the Managua

Intercontinental Hotel.
As one tried to reach the command post in an army convoy, driving over streets strewn with concrete and glass and trying to avoid collapsing walls, looters were already ravaging the stores and bodies protruded from the rubble. Over the next forty years, I made dozens of medical and humanitarian trips to all areas of the country, and, as will be seen in this section, the initial medical focus merged into a diplomatic and philosophic journey into the heart of a tortured land.

Nicaragua

*For 25 years I owned a home in Nicaragua, a commitment made in
1985 during the Contra-Sandinista War; I never slept in
the house. At first it was used as a residence for volunteer doctors
and nurses; later it became an art gallery organized by a
priest-friend. As these articles indicate, my early service there was
in an earthquake shattered city, living with the then President.
As I came to know the country I grew very sympathetic to the
aspirations of the oppressed, and during the 1980s spent much time
there with my wife trying to establish a health service and using
the credibility of medicine to foster peace. In retrospect, my efforts
failed to change the course of events, but these articles remain
my testament to the rights of a small nation, and to what I believe
the United States should properly represent.*

The Nicaraguan Earthquake
The U.S. Congressional Record, 1973

In the middle of Managua several days after the major earthquake had struck on December 23, 1972, I stood with an old American Army sergeant who, looking at the total destruction of the city, the flames and smoke billowing from still collapsing structures, the rending noise of walls giving way and the constant sound of sirens, with the acrid odor of dead and burning flesh hanging heavy – this old, tired, dirty, career soldier said two things: "God, but it feels good to be an American soldier" and "Even Dresden and Berlin in 1945 weren't as bad as this." In a sense, those are two of the themes of this report.

Shortly after the earthquake struck Managua, with maximal reading of 6.7 on the Richter scale, I was called by the ambassador of Nicaragua to the United Nations who requested that I direct their crippled health service. There were almost no facts available at that time regarding the extent of the damage or the needs, and useful planning in such a vacuum, was virtually impossible. Although contact was established by ham radio shortly after the quake, conflicting and often contradictory reports came; the only unquestioned fact was that this was a disaster in a capital city without parallel in the Western hemisphere.

A series of preliminary tremors shook Managua starting about 10:00 at night on December 22 and culminating in several major tremors between 12:30 and 4:30 on the morning of December 23. Many of those who experienced the full intensity of the tremors in the center of Managua are not alive to describe that occurrence, since the majority of the buildings instantaneously collapsed. However, one did not have to search far anywhere in Managua to find those with tales of miraculous survival coupled with great tragedy.

The buildings were literally lifted off the ground, shifted, and came back with a thud, collapsing the plaster, wood, cement, and packed mud that made up the foundation of so many of the common houses. Fires, breaking out throughout town, provided the only light since all electricity was instantly knocked out. Water mains burst, and flooding from the surrounding lakes occurred in low-lying areas. Managua is set in a frame of volcanic hills, and landslides buried many. The roads were crosshatched with the crevices of a fissured earth and were covered with the rubble of collapsing buildings, live electric wires, dead and injured people.

Even several days later the emotional paralysis of the stunned citizenry was striking: I saw a family sitting on the lawn of their destroyed home in the midst of a block of burning buildings while they guarded their damaged furniture, including all the Christmas decorations that were about to be used when the quake struck. In fact, throughout Managua the eye was caught by the striking contrast of Christmas themes and devastation. As one of the tallest buildings in Managua burned out of control, one could see a line of multicolored Christmas lights dangling from the upper floors, with the Star of Hope, framed in billowing smoke, as the main street burned to the ground. The red glow of Managua dying is a scene I shall never forget.

Immediately after the disaster the first priority was to find the wounded and to care for them, and then try to find the dead and bury them before they became a further threat, as a focus of disease, for the living. To complicate this enormous medical challenge, it should be noted that the two major hospitals in Managua, with seventeen hundred acute care beds, were totally destroyed in the earthquake. There were, therefore, no medical facilities remaining in the area.

The initial response from the United States of America was rapid and massive. Within twelve hours after the first report a team of twenty-five physicians and medical corpsmen from the American army base in the Panama Canal Zone were working on the front lawn of what had been the General Hospital in Managua. Within twenty-four hours a twenty-five bed hospital was functioning, and within another twenty-four hours, a further hundred bed American military hospital with four operating theaters was providing the only major surgical care. Water purification equipment was flown in within the first two days and distribution of water and food supplies to the populace was begun.

In some ways the response of the United States of America to the Nicaraguan earthquake was in the finest tradition of our country. The enormous power, organization, and efficiency of the United States employed with such immediacy for a devastated city and a damaged population was in keeping with what most Americans think is our heritage. Around the world, however, too many people see only another aspect of the United States' power. It was a beautiful experience to be an American in Managua in the last week of 1972 and to know that our only impact overseas is not being felt in Hanoi or Hai Phong. More than any other impression I brought back from Nicaragua was the conviction that this type of activity is a role through which our great country can contribute to the world.

The private side of America—voluntary agencies and individuals of good will—have a great role to play. There was, however, no coordination of their activities in the disaster in Nicaragua. In fact, it often seemed their presence was either resented or ignored by the United States Embassy and military.

While I firmly believe that only the American military could have responded to the immediate need and to the scope of the Nicaraguan earthquake, I am equally convinced that their prolonged presence there will be a mistake. After the first several weeks, or even a month, the casualties will have healed and gone their way, and the chore of rebuilding a new Nicaragua will be primarily a Nicaraguan task. The remarkable thing about a military hospital is that it comes self-contained with trained personnel who work among themselves with startling efficiency. As time goes on, however, that system just does not work well in an alien culture.

For example, it is common in many tropical counties, including Nicaragua, for families to stay by the bedside of an injured person, to cook for and nurse the patient. This practice is inconsistent with the routine of a military hospital, where the flow of civilian population is markedly restricted. One could see the steady increase in emotional pressure at the hospital gate and the inevitable rise in tension resulting from a foreign military controlling every aspect of daily life. Within a few days after the earthquake it also became apparent that some of the Nicaraguan physicians wanted to utilize the American military hospital.

At this time, it seems desirable to leave our portable medical facility there. Eventually, however, one must ask for how long will it be a good thing – or even possible – to have an organized, rigid military system working at one level of competency in daily contact with another less efficient but more permanent approach? In fact, I think it almost guarantees a rapid abrasion of feelings. As soon as the immediate crisis is over, it is my belief that the American military presence in a foreign nation's medical system ought to terminate.

The Price for Differing With the U.S. Is Death
Newsday, 1987

The fat lady with severe asthma couldn't breathe and the "Baby Bird," a pediatric machine that was the sole respirator functioning in the largest hospital in Managua, offered only symbolic help. There were six adult respirators in the eight bed intensive care unit at the Manolo Morales Hospital, but all were broken. The U.S. economic embargo against Nicaragua has interrupted the supply of essential spare parts and prevented the purchase of new machines.

In Nicaragua the price for differing with the United States is death; the Contra War is the major direct cause of adult morbidity and mortality, and even the innocent asthmatic dies because of our misguided policies. There are no sheets or blankets in most medical wards in Managua. There are few bandages and only makeshift splints at the Aldo Chavarria Rehabilitation Hospital. Three weeks ago, I examined dozens of legless victims of Contra mines at this sprawling series of tin roofed sheds that has been converted into one of the busiest hospitals in Nicaragua. The numbers of new amputees outpace the capacity of the three technicians who produce simple wooden limbs. When I made clinical rounds in this hospital six months ago, I examined many of the same patients, and their innocent eyes held an eloquent condemnation I cannot escape.

The diagnostic equipment we take for granted in the United States no longer exists in Managua. Maybe five percent of the microscopes are intact. One cannot measure blood gas levels in any hospital. They have few functioning x-ray machines, but then again almost no x-ray film or developing fluids are available. The more sophisticated scanning equipment has not functioned in years because it is impossible to obtain American spare parts. Almost all of the modern medical equipment in Nicaragua is of U.S. manufacture. But since compassion and generosity do not appear to be highly rated qualities in our current breed of heroes and leaders, these machines are likely to remain broken, and more Nicaraguans will die. There is currently an adequate supply of insulin and anti-tuberculosis drugs, thanks to European donors, but vaccines and blood products spoil because the scientific freezers are broken.

One of the most impressive aspects of the medical picture in Nicaragua is the simple presence of doctors and nurses. Medical personnel are easy migrants, for their skills find a ready market. The fact that they remain at their posts, trying to improvise in a steadily deteriorating setting, speaks volumes for the eight year old and ongoing revolution. They stay because they are now part of a national experiment in which the wealth of a previously servile nation has been spread among peasants who were illiterate and had never seen a doctor.

They stay because of deeply spiritual reasons, because they have witnessed a theology that espouses a preferential option for the poor, translated into an unparalleled government program of land grants for campesinos who had known only a life of indentured servitude under previous American supported regimes. They stay, ultimately, because it is their country, with all its warts, and they will not surrender their independence. Our politics of death and destruction are destined to fail because Nicaraguans have tasted freedom and will no longer grovel with a banana republic mentality.

A hospital offers a wonderful cross section of a community, mirroring in its halls and wards not the political rhetoric of statesmen or warriors, but the dreams of a society as well as the realities of a land in conflict and an economy in shambles.

The overwhelming impression, at least to this physician who has regularly worked in Nicaragua for fifteen years, is one of a deepening strength and determination. There is an almost palpable pride that permeates the Managua medical scene – and survival, not surrender, is their future.

We, the most powerful nation on earth, a country built by those who fled oppression, should understand Nicaragua's right to be free. Our American heritage was not built on conquering the weak; armed intervention in other lands is alien to the democratic traditions we cherish. Yet we, the United States of America, have been convicted in the International Court of Justice of supporting terrorism, mining harbors, and killing and maiming innocent civilians in Nicaragua. The Contra forces are a shameful creation of American administration policy.

To invoke the words used recently by a lieutenant colonel with a distorted sense of history, "for the love of God and the love of our country," let us cease killing and begin to foster healing and peace.

Of Constitutions, Democracy, Medicine, and Diplomacy
The New York Times, 1987

Thomas Jefferson would be at ease in Nicaragua today. He understood the need for both revolution and an authentic Constitution. Of revolution, Jefferson said, "I hold it that a little rebellion now and then is a good thing, and as necessary in the political world as storms in the physical… It is a medicine necessary for the sound health of government." Having known armed struggle, this philosopher of national freedom, the author of the U.S. Declaration of Independence, the champion of man's innate claims to life, liberty, and the pursuit of happiness, participated in drafting a Constitution that would guide his new nation.

But unlike those who see all other forms of government as a mortal threat, Jefferson believed that "Nothing is unchangeable but the inherent and inalienable rights of man." He noted, "Some men look at Constitutions with sanctimonious reverence and deem them like the Ark of the Covenant, too sacred to be touched. They ascribe to men of the preceding age a wisdom more than human and suppose what they did to be beyond amendment… I know that laws and Constitutions must go hand in hand with the progress of the human mind… Each generation has the right to choose for itself the form of government it believes the most promotive of its own happiness."

Today, Nicaragua has a new Constitution and an ongoing revolution. The mood, however, is hardly one of national celebration. The major concern is how to understand and deal with a United States administration that is openly committed to overthrowing the Nicaraguan government. I believe such an illicit policy and such immoral behavior underestimates not only the Nicaraguan, but the American public.

For two hundred years, the mainstream of America has understood, and always returned to, the fundamentals of Jeffersonian thought. Whenever we had a coherent foreign policy, it was not based merely upon reaction or fear, but upon the ideas and ideals that Thomas Jefferson expounded. Abraham Lincoln, always succinct, noted simply that "the principles of Jefferson are the definition of a free society."

An apparent ignorance of our own history, coupled with a cynical and arrogant abuse of false power—false because its foundation is nothing more than shifting expediency—has now tarnished our Jeffersonian image at home as well as abroad. It is difficult for Americans to understand how Israeli raids against Lebanese camps can be justified as appropriate defensive measures against terrorist threats while Nicaragua is condemned for pursuing armed bands that have killed and maimed thirty five thousand of its citizens in the past five years. It is also difficult for the average American to understand how our present administration, drawing its power from a Constitution that mandates separation of church and state can dictate such an involvement in Nicaragua as a price for stopping armed assault.

Fortunately, the unreal world of false and bizarre images finally seems to be collapsing. Sordid deals and duplicitous leaders replace even mercenary "freedom fighters" as the investigative spotlight exposes our national folly and shame. Jefferson and Lincoln would have understood—"You can fool some of the people all of the time and all of the people some of the time. But you can't fool all of the people all of the time." Today, senior members of both parties in the U.S. Congress and the vast majority of the polled electorate, openly dissent from an official policy based on covert operations and demand a return to open government.

There is controversy and confusion in the United States regarding many aspects of Nicaraguan life, but the average American understands and appreciates their struggle against oppression and corruption; he can understand a campaign that decreased the illiteracy rate from an appalling 50.3 percent to less than thirteen percent and reduced by a third the infant mortality rate.

Nicaragua's traditions and problems are different from ours, but we share the same inalienable right to life, liberty, and the pursuit of happiness. These are not national perquisites that come with power but are understood by the average American to be universal, fundamental, and nonnegotiable claims of humanity. Without this assumption, democracy makes no sense, and if we, as a nation, abandon this concept, we have lost our bearings and our "morality," a word Jefferson also emphasized in his dreams for America. It is a morality that is rooted in accepting the freedom and inherent equality of all men. The amoral will neither understand nor defend these rights and will, cynically, pursue only their own self-interests. One must, however, have confidence that two hundred years of Jeffersonian approach will eventually prevail.

For the past thirty-five years, I have been fortunate to serve, usually in the midst of chaos and crisis, the sick, the frightened, the poor, and the hungry of Africa, Latin America, the Middle East, and Asia. I realized very quickly that neither politicians nor soldiers nor diplomats had a monopoly on wisdom in foreign affairs. My journeys were rarely to resorts, but then again, very little that really matters in a world filled with change and conflict ever happens in resorts. I have just returned from Nicaragua, where I spent my time at a field hospital in a war zone and at a rehabilitation center in Managua. I was seared by the pain of groups of mothers whose sons had been mutilated and killed by our mercenary forces.

Our official obsession with the policy of overthrowing the Sandinista government at any cost has not only caused obvious violations of Congressional intent but has isolated us from a world that believes in the independence and sovereignty of individual nations. We have been ordered by the court to "cease and refrain" from Contra support and to pay reparations, and yet we persist in our aggression.

Fortunately, the administration's approach is at least partly balanced by the thousands of Americans serving Nicaraguans in their struggle for independence. There are more American teachers in Nicaraguan schools than Russians and Cubans combined. American farmers, architects, scientists, and artists have become regular features of Nicaraguan life.

A physician may have the most privileged role. The intense and intimate relationships of doctor and patient force both parties to an understanding that is unique; trust and love can evolve in days and be remembered for years. When people and nations can agree on little else, those common bonds become the bridge back to understanding and peace. There should also be no conflict in combining the healing roles of a physician and citizen. Six of the signers of Jefferson's Declaration of Independence were physicians, and that precedent may offer a path of hope in the midst of conflict such as is now destroying Nicaragua.

A new Constitution has now been proclaimed in Nicaragua in the midst of war. Friendship and understanding must replace suspicion and hatred as we recall, in the spirit of Jefferson, that the rule of law and the liberties of mankind are what we must all strive for if peace is ever to return to our troubled world. Those basic tenets of civilized society apply to the powerful as well as the weak. At the beginning of the century, the great Nicaraguan poet, Rubén Darío wrote:

"I seek a form that my style cannot discover
a bud of thought that wants to be a rose."

Americans should understand and support this dream.

Holidays in Nicaragua
America, 1988

It was difficult to find reasons for celebration this past Thanksgiving in Nicaragua. Even the Misquito Indians, returning from refugee camps in Honduras, were delayed, and my romantic plans for dinner with them never materialized. I doubt that anything has ever been on time in Puerto Cabezas. Thanksgiving is a uniquely American holiday, and citizens living overseas normally parade their identity and share, in a symbolic meal, their good fortune. In Nicaragua today, there are few reasons for joy; to be an American there on Thanksgiving was almost embarrassing. The U.S.-supported Contra forces continue to murder, rape, and terrorize, while the national economy has collapsed under our embargo. The signs of death, destruction, and abject poverty are everywhere – hardly the setting for a Thanksgiving feast.

Yet traditions are important in our lives, and only a sense of history and a belief in the mercy of God made this Thanksgiving Day tolerable. I left the capital city of Managua – where I had been attempting to resurrect, for the government, a health system crippled by war – and traveled to the Atlantic coast town of Puerto Cabezas.

Prosperity is a relative term, and there are few surprises for a tropical medicine specialist who has worked in numerous refugee camps during the past thirty years. But the initial – and lasting – impression of Puerto Cabezas is one of long suffering tinged by perverse incongruities and life saving humor. Nature and war have been unkind parents.

It is a town of ramshackle wooden houses set on stilts over a malarious marsh. There is no running water, no telephone, no television, only occasional and sparse electrical service, and no fire department. Conflagrations fanned by the Atlantic winds seem to be a regular phenomenon that the local population accepts as part of their fate. There is one paved street. At the intersection near the school hangs a huge traffic light. It doesn't work, but the town leaders are very proud of it and believe it symbolizes urban progress to the Indian tribes that come in to trade from the Rio Coco and its tributaries.

Clinical rounds in the local hospital offered the best insight into the reality – and courage – of Puerto Cabezas. A tin roofed shed, built 75 years ago, houses those desperate enough to seek medical care. I had a bizarre conversation with a German-born surgeon who firmly refused "to operate any more without anesthesia; they move too much, I just can't do it." Since the U.S. economic embargo went into effect five years ago, there are chronic shortages in every sector of society, but nowhere can the impact be felt more clearly than at the hospital.

Shortages of bandages and plaster make homemade casts and traction splints worthy of a Rube Goldberg. The intensive care unit appeared to be so designated because there were two blood pressure cuffs and a fan; there was no other equipment in the room. Tuberculosis is rampant, but appropriate drugs are in short supply. The antibiotics we take for granted do not exist in the real world of Puerto Cabezas. There mothers and babies die of treatable infections because a U.S. President wants Nicaragua to "cry uncle."

The Reagan Administration apparently believes that our government, sprung from Pilgrims who once shared their bounty with Indians, has somehow inherited the right to dictate how others should live. If the poor and hungry and diseased citizens of Nicaragua do not accept our direction then, according to our current leaders, it is justified in unleashing mercenary forces to murder and destroy in the name of democracy.

Returning to Managua thinking of the next holiday we are already planning in our safe and comfortable society, I could only hope that history will be kind to us. Maybe future scholars will recall that while misguided politicians inflicted terrible pain on innocent women and children and severely tarnished our own traditions, thousands of American volunteers came to Central America. Farmers and contractors, clergy and medical workers, young enthusiasts and retirees who lost their own children in Vietnam give witness today in Nicaragua to the American heritage we like to recall at Thanksgiving and Christmas.

There is a movement for peace throughout Central America, but it demands that we stop supporting the Contra rebels. One can no longer indulge in the obscene – and deadly – game of defining helicopters and military training as humanitarian aid. We must recapture the true spirit of America, one built on tolerance, understanding and a sharing of our wealth with those less fortunate – regardless of their color, or religion, or traditions.

We must give peace a chance to take seed in the rubble we have created in Nicaragua. There may be, if we allow it to happen, a Second Coming during this Christmas season when, to paraphrase Yeats, peace like a rough beast, its hour come round at last, slouches toward Bethlehem to be born.

Fasting and Medicine in Nicaragua
America, 1985

Medicine is a rare profession, possibly the only one that can permit immediate and total access where suspicion and even hostility might be expected. Deep national differences do not divide the physician and the patient, and the bridge to understanding that seems so elusive for politicians and diplomats caught in an endless power game may be found in the common concerns of shared pain, suffering, and healing.

This conviction that medicine offers a rare opportunity for international diplomacy was set forth in *The Untapped Resource* (1971), published by Maryknoll's Orbis Books. I was the author, and the Rev. Miguel D'Escoto, M. M., was the publisher.

Now he is Foreign Minister of Nicaragua, and I, an American physician, was trying to manage the medical complications of his almost month long total fast. Father D'Escoto had been drinking only water in a spiritual exercise he hoped would call attention to the effects of American foreign policy on his nation. The thesis we had developed so passionately fourteen years earlier now offered a personal opportunity for implementation. The level of mutual misunderstanding and inflammatory rhetoric seen in recent U.S.-Nicaraguan communications faded as I measured falling blood pressure and decreasing urinary output. Mixed in with discussions on the effects of starvation were dialogues on the meanings of freedom, democracy, and independence.

The stethoscope was a symbol of decency and offered a key to an embattled land, where a young government was attempting to deal in its own independent fashion with inherited problems of poverty, ignorance, and disease unrivaled in Central America. The trust, confidence and gratitude that greeted me might be attributed to my medical services in Nicaragua. But I would suspect that it reflected a more universal desire for peace with dignity, a preference for dialogue rather than destruction, and a belief that tolerance, even generosity, should be expected from a great nation dealing with a determined and proud but poor, and admittedly inexperienced, government.

Between visits to Father D'Escoto, I had hours of conversation with President Daniel Ortega and met spiritual leaders – bishops, priests, and nuns – from all over Latin America who were fasting in union with Father D'Escoto. Something profound was happening in that simple church shed with its unpainted corrugated roof and leaking walls. Embodied in the frame of a fasting priest were the frustrations and bitterness of long oppressed campesinos and others who fought for their basic human rights. Mixed with the stagnant smell of a tropical sick room was the warm perfume of love. A confidence that the aspirations of Latin America were about to be realized permeated the congregation.

It may be difficult to measure the force that emanates from such a gathering, but I suspect the changing political winds sweeping Peru and Uruguay, Brazil and Argentina have been further fanned by the fast of Miguel D'Escoto, and they will not fade. The spiritual tool so effectively used by Gandhi was again unifying downtrodden peoples across parochial borders. In understanding and serving the dreams of the starving, we may find solutions – or at least approaches – where traditional methods have failed.

The RCSI is a venerable Dublin institution founded in 1784. It is the most international medical school in the western world, with a student body from over thirty nations. A mosque in the basement allows Islamic students to pray towards Mecca via a central Dublin park. I trained over 4,000 undergraduates and hundreds of postdoctoral specialists in my thirty-six

years as Chairman of the Department of Tropical Medicine and International Health. The College is endowed with ancient traditions and lovingly restored public areas—the site of many memorable dinners, with rich talk, fine wines, and the establishment of lasting friendships. Very soon after my appointment in 1969 as Professor, I began to meet Irish poets and novelists, artists and architects, and they, even more than my medical colleagues, made my Dublin stays periods of great joy. Once a year, Kate and I sponsored a non-medical lecture, and here, in the front foyer of the school, with the statues of long dead surgeons looking on, my old and dear friend, the poet Seamus Heaney, and I discussed the meaning and beauty of words.

Ireland

For thirty-six years I served as Professor and Chairman of a Department in an Irish medical school and began a transatlantic commute that anchored our life in Dublin as well as New York. I also served for four decades as the President-General of the American Irish Historical Society, and used that platform to extend my arguments for freedom from the Middle East, Africa, and Latin America to the land of my ancestors. These articles were written in reaction to the armed conflict that I personally observed in Northern Ireland in the late 1960s and throughout the 1970s and 1980s until peace came through the Good Friday Agreements in 1998.

A Perverse Silence
New York Daily News, 1979

There was a time, eons ago, when Celtic myths were new and the secrets of Irish life found expression in heroic figures. The characters of The Tain were used in ancient times to capture the hard realities of life in a cold, rough island adrift off the west coast of Europe. The mysteries of love and combat and death were molded into tales that still thrive in Ireland. This survival is due, in part, to the Irish love of words and talk, but it also reflects the harsh fact that the past, particularly the violent sins of the past, still dominates the present in parts of that lovely land.

The myths and symbols of the druids and bards are now misused to justify terrorism, as if a new generation of Irish had no other option than to repeat the primordial acts of bloodletting and human sacrifice. The hills of Ulster, which once thundered with the roar of Cuchulainn's battle chariot, today echo with the sounds of strife and bitterness, with the modern clamor of gunfire and plastic explosives. Such scenes, enchanting as they might be in ancient history or mythology, are a tragedy to those who live them and a shame to those who witness them in silence.

That is why, in a recent newspaper article I spoke out once again to draw American and international attention to Northern Ireland—a subdivision of Eire unknown to the ancient Celts and unworkable for the modern. With colleagues I sought to identify with the innocent victims of Belfast fighting for "a life before death in Northern Ireland."

We called upon the United States to encourage Britain to plan conscientiously now for what seems inevitable to most observers—a future in which the island of Ireland will be governed only by the Irish. We suggested a series of specific acts that the United States could take to promote peace and justice in Northern Ireland now.

We called upon the American press and other media to educate our citizens about Northern Ireland, to show not only the horrible impact of continuous violence; but also to focus on the hope for peace that lies in the courage and tenacity of those political leaders who have worked so long to establish an equitable system of government.

British politicians reacted quickly and strongly to this article, denouncing the impropriety of foreign intervention into what they claim is an internal matter. England has, since the article, had a national election and a new party is now in power. But for Northern Ireland, nothing seems to change. A conspiracy of silence and perverse political neglect is the apparent policy of the day. In the Queen's thirty minute address to the new Parliament, the topic of Northern Ireland rated twenty seconds. Our own government did not react officially at all. Nothing has happened since, except a mindless continuation of the daily body count published in some obscure corner of the Ulster newspapers.

It is almost as though the subject is taboo. In the Irish myths, there is an element of primitive magic called the *geis*—an absolute prohibition from doing certain things. Somehow, in mythology, that can make sense. But in the reality of today, it is difficult to imagine what *geis* has been applied that prevents our government and our press from being involved in, or even talking about, Northern Ireland.

There has been ample documentation of violations of human rights in Ulster, especially in its detention centers. The evidence has come not only from the oppressed themselves, but from Amnesty International, the European Court of Human Rights, Protestant prison physicians, and even an official British government report.

The Catholic minority in the North exists under an historical burden of gross social and economic discriminations and still has no effective political power. The majority Unionist Party adamantly refuses to consider any power sharing. And the British government, using a remarkably circular logic, reasons that it can do nothing to bring about a political solution until the majority party in Northern Ireland, which it created, agrees.

Is it some sort of magic *geis* that strikes our government dumb in the face of this intolerable situation, when it is so willing to speak out strongly on Rhodesia and Russia and Nicaragua and Ghana?

Or is Ireland somehow a victim of its own mythology and folklore? Are we doomed to believe that this "most distressful country" will ever be such; that Deirdre is doomed to destroy herself, that Kathleen ni Houlihan will never be released from the grip of sadness and tragedy? Certainly, there is a fairly widespread notion in this country that nothing will ever change in Northern Ireland. People say: "It's been going on for four hundred years and will probably go on for another four hundred." This sort of intellectual evasion springs, no doubt, from the complexity of Irish history, both ancient and modern, and a willingness to follow a mental course of least resistance. The problems in Ulster are complex. They are deeply rooted in political, religious, and ethnic differences and will not yield to simplistic solutions. But that cannot be an excuse for inactivity. Where would we be today if, in the early 1960s, the legislators of our country had decided that racial discrimination had gone on for two hundred years and would probably continue for another two hundred? We have not yet realized the ideal of equality embodied in our laws, but we have made a start.

That is what is needed today in Northern Ireland – to make a start, to break the stalemate. I contend, once again, that our government has an obligation to use its influence in motivating Britain to begin to seek a resolution that will offer political equality to all of Ireland.

American intervention in other troubled areas of the world has been too frequently based on financing one faction or the other. Our record of success with this approach has certainly not been very good, and more and more Americans are realizing the cold immorality of contributing to bloodshed in a safely distant country.

Equally insidious, however, is our apparently selective inactivity and the puzzling unwillingness of a great and powerful nation to condemn repetitive violations of basic human rights in Ireland. The failure to speak out unequivocally against these wrongs and to use our enormous influence to secure peace amounts to a condoning of injustice and hatred, to sharing in the waste of young, innocent lives, and to the imprisonment of the elderly in chains of fear.

There are no innocent bystanders when human rights are at stake. Those who are aware of the terrible wrongs in Northern Ireland and remain silent are guilty of prolonging the tragedy. Those who let themselves be daunted by the complexity are guilty of an intellectual timidity akin to moral cowardice. Those who could lead but choose to confine their efforts to their own problems and to ignore a brother in need are guilty, to say the least, of a lack of charity.

We do not pretend to have all the answers. We cannot, like Finn McCool, eat the salmon from the river Boyne and thereby gain all knowledge. Nor do we wish to impose any particular solution. But this small—and in today's scale of value, globally insignificant—country has a call upon our conscience that we should not neglect. Ireland has made a vast contribution to our country that we cannot forget. We should not dismiss the people of Northern Ireland, Protestant or Catholic, merely because their numbers are small or because their struggle is embarrassing to England, a nation for whom we have been a willing ally in wars and a desired friend in peace.

We must continue to condemn the futile, self-destructive terrorism of the IRA and to warn against any American support for those emissaries of violence with their politics of death. But, far more importantly, we must try to promote American economic incentives that offer hope for a decent life in Northern Ireland and the basis for a lasting, viable peace in a land that is still caught in the web of her sad history and ancient myths.

Red Stains on the Emerald Isle: Can Only Blood Wash Them Out?
The New York Times, 1984

There is a blood red strand—dark and evil—that runs through the tapestry of Irish history. Amid the soft hues of saints and scholars, side by side with the rich colors of bards and poets, are streaks of violence, torn threads representing sudden death and wanton destruction.

That perverse part of the Irish scene is perpetuated today, not merely by fanatics, intent on imposing their own peculiar view of justice through the barrel of a gun or the blast of a hidden bomb, or even by those simplistic partisans who, far from danger, glorify killing and romanticize guerrilla warfare. The greatest guilt lies with the failed political leadership on both sides of the Atlantic. Successive Dublin governments have underestimated the deep interest of many American Irish in the current tragedy in Northern Ireland. Instead of mobilizing the vast potential of immigrant goodwill to help resolve the wrongs in Belfast and Derry, Dublin politicians seem to restrict their contact in this country to an endless series of condemnations of American Irish financial contributions.

If some of America's hard earned, generously offered dollars have gone to the "wrong hands" in Northern Ireland, the major blame, I would suggest, lies in the unimaginative policymakers of Dublin. They deceive themselves that pandering to a few American politicians is an adequate substitute for establishing working relations with interested academic, religious, athletic, and cultural organizations in this country. While Israel has carefully courted international involvement in her struggle for freedom and security, the Republic of Ireland, a nation of comparable size and population, has taken an opposite tack, denying her own internal troubles and arrogantly dismissing American concerns.

In a recent poll, less than 1 percent of the Republic's citizens even listed the conflict in Northern Ireland as a primary problem, and local politicians, faithful to their standards, have not led the masses toward peace. They have sought refuge in the tragic status quo. The American Irish community has been no more fortunate in the political leadership offered by its elected officials. In a land where the Speaker of the House of Representatives and numerous senior senators and leading governors are of Irish extraction, one might have expected some evidence of their influence on government programs aimed at resolving the longest lasting guerrilla war in Western Europe.

Other ethnic groups do not hesitate to use their political clout. Almost fifty percent of all American foreign aid goes to Israel; virtually none goes to Ireland. Preferential federal legislation permits the transfer of some $750 million a year in tax exempt charitable contributions to Israel, and other laws permit almost ninety-five percent of Israel's exports to enter the United States duty free. Military subsidies and other grants to Israel cost the American taxpayer billions of dollars annually. There is no similar assistance available to promote Ireland's exports or alleviate her security costs. Approved programs for charitable donations by American Irish to their homeland are almost nonexistent. American politicians of Irish origin do not seem to share the same ethnic pride or interest in their ancestral home as that which motivates their Jewish Congressional colleagues. Annual St. Patrick's Day statements are simply no substitute for concrete acts of assistance.

There are ample precedents to justify a helpful American involvement in the present tragedy in Northern Ireland. In a *Foreign Policy* article several years ago, I offered specific proposals based on established government programs in other parts of the world, where technical assistance, cultural exchange, security supports, and bank and tax credits to promote American investment have all been used to hasten peace in troubled lands. Such programs could – and should – win the same ecumenical support enjoyed by those who have so successfully asked our assistance for Israel and other countries.

The American Irish community, working in the vacuum created by Dublin and Washington, has failed to channel its emotions into an effective pressure force. Many are unaware of the brutality of everyday life in an area where prejudice, oppression, paranoia, and fear distort every facet of existence. Too many American Irish carry on their passionate fights with a courage untouched by personal experience and, far from the carnage, use words and donations that only prolong the agony of those caught in the maelstrom of hatred that flourishes in the ghettos of Northern Ireland today.

There is nothing noble in the killing and maiming of innocent people, or even in the sad waste of the young who take their own lives. Romantic rhetoric cannot excuse indiscriminate violence or justify the sordid obsession in Northern Ireland with useless sacrifice and almost ritual bloodletting.

In contrast with many Americans who glibly comment on the origins and solution of the "troubles" in the north, I have had the unique privilege of teaching medicine in Ireland four times a year for the last fifteen years. My own perspective on Northern Ireland is tempered by a clinician's experience with suffering and pain and by a deep belief that the very permanence of death solves nothing.

I have shared days with fellow physicians in the emergency rooms of Belfast, known colleagues whose children have been killed by the "brave lads" because their fathers dared to care for the wounds of the enemy, and seen the destruction of a generation etched in the pinched, suspicious faces of women in the Falls Road and Ardoyne ghettos.

From a purely pragmatic point of view, one must reject the failed guerrilla policies of force as well as the Republic's politics of denial. We must emulate the Jewish community and learn to lobby in a forceful manner, so that American politicians will no longer think their obligations are fulfilled by issuing fatuous St. Patrick's Day pronouncements.

It is time that the American Irish unified their efforts to tear out those blood red, dark and evil strands of violence that scar the Irish dream and to initiate cooperative projects that can bring jobs, dignity, and peace to a long-suffering land.

A Deathless Dream
Journal of the Royal College of Surgeons in Ireland, 1969

Not far from here in a small cell in Mountjoy jail during "The Troubles" one inmate summarized the basic ingredients of Ireland's struggle for independence – "a few men faithful and a deathless dream." That is all it really takes for any great movement, and Ireland has been endowed throughout her history with her few faithful men and many dreams.

I intend to articulate an approach in international medicine that not only befits Ireland's heritage, but is necessary and will become inevitable in the 1970s and in the decades to come. The concepts and tentative programs I shall discuss will not be realized this year, or the next, or even the next, but it is well that we have a goal. It is well that we reflect on the changing approach necessary to accomplish the deathless dream of medicine – that of bringing health to mankind in all lands regardless of race or creed or color. When President John F. Kennedy spoke before the Irish Parliament he urged this approach, quoting George Bernard Shaw: "Some people see things as they are and ask why; I dream things that never were and ask why not?"

Ireland has had a long, proud involvement in tropical medicine. For many centuries her missionaries have gone abroad, combining the healing arts with their own attempt at religious persuasion, and one could travel the length and breadth of Africa today and never be too far from the lilt of an Irish brogue. The cold, salty breezes of the Liffey must refresh the minds of physicians around the world who have studied in this College, and now labor in the stifling jungles of Africa or in the hot, humid cities of Asia. The founder of modern tropical medicine, Sir Patrick Manson, would periodically rejuvenate his spirit at, and eventually retire to, Lough Mask in Galway, where his fishing lodge, The Sheiling, became the repository of so much that was fine and good in the early efforts of this century in international medicine. It's almost ironic, if somewhat blasphemous, to recall that The Sheiling was destroyed in a bit of anti British feeling in 1922.

Ireland's heritage in international medicine and world affairs has been one of quality, if not quantity. It has been one of men who, like James Joyce, left these shores and, laboring overseas, brought great credit back to the motherland. Today, Ireland can be, as President Kennedy so aptly phrased it, "a maker and shaper of world peace." She has none of the historical and political burdens of the superpowers; she is acceptable to the sensitive developing lands of the world; her army has been called upon by the UN to serve in Africa, in the Middle East, and in Cyprus.

For all these reasons and also because Ireland promotes itself, and properly so, as the center for international medical education, with students coming to this Royal College of Surgeons from thirty three nations, and as the home of the largest missionary network in the world, there must be a greater recognition that the standard approaches in medical education aimed at producing Irish physicians for the small towns of this wonderful land or even for the sophisticated centers of Dublin are no longer enough. There must be a change in goals, and in dreams, and in curriculum that will reflect the modern role that is uniquely Ireland's today. The problems of the vast hordes of malnourished, poverty stricken, parasite ridden peoples around the world are by choice, and certainly by default, Ireland's problems.

When William Butler Yeats criticized the flamboyance of *The Silver Tassie*, author Sean O'Casey wrote to him stating, "That is exactly, in my opinion, what most dramatists are trying to do, building up little worlds of wallpaper and hiding striding life behind it." We of this College—and I associate myself proudly with you tonight—cannot avoid the strident, flamboyant, exciting, depressing, and sometimes overwhelming problems of life in the tropics today. It is necessary not merely to offer the charitable crumbs of your table after the fact, but to willingly accept this new role as the educational leader of international medicine.

Such adaptation has occurred here in the past. Preventive medicine, the very basis for international health, realized its first formal chair in this College in 1841, and what I propose is merely a continuation of that thinking. The tropics intruded upon this College even earlier than 1841. When I was reading Professor Widdess's book on the history of this institution, it was of interest to note that, in 1821, a stuffed giraffe stood at the bottom of the main staircase. Now I can't promise that, if you heed my words tonight, we shall have such lusty signs of tropical medicine in our foyer again, but I can tell you that a program of excellence in international medicine that will grow year after year is possible.

A College owes an obligation to the people it has trained; those graduates deserve your collaboration. You need their facilities for future training. And, once again, you have assumed a role that you must now fulfill.

When I married my wife she gave me a silver inkwell inscribed with a phrase by Sean O'Casey: "Its time we paint our own pictures, pictures that are good enough to hang in the hallway." Your pictures have been good enough to hang in the hallway for many years, and I suggest, as the first step, that this fact be appreciated and utilized.

Medicine is an untapped resource in international diplomacy, and Ireland, more than any other nation in the world today, must make use of this resource. Ireland, with the goodwill it has built over many years in the tropics, must take a lead in training the modern physicians of the coming decades. The world has changed utterly, and the young in Irish medicine need—and will demand—an international training equivalent to that required by their colleagues from foreign lands. There is no single or simple system to satisfy this need, and different disciplines and talents must be brought to bear.

Ireland has come of age in international medicine, with obligations and responsibilities and opportunities that must be fulfilled. It has a heritage in tropical medicine that deserves continuation. It has a history of courage and adaptation that will assure this continuity. The coming decades will put a burden upon this land. To serve the emerging nations as few other nations have ever been able, you have the educational talents and the institutional arrangements necessary to permit the development of an international medical program.

President Kennedy, on leaving these shores, declared: "I am going to come back to see old Shannon's face again. This is not the land of my birth but is the land for which I have the greatest affection." I think you may realize that you have me for good. The Atlantic shall not be the bitter bowl of tears it was to Joyce, but a transient obstacle in this jet age effort to link Ireland and the United States via the tropics. I intend to work for the dream, the deathless dream that I have articulated. I don't expect it to come easily or quickly but come it must.

An Irish poet wrote of the links between Ireland and America as follows:

We, in the ages lying
In the buried past of the earth
Built Nineveh with our sighing
And Babel itself with our mirth;
And o'erthrew them with prophesying
To the old of the New World's worth
For each age is a dream that is dying
Or one that is coming to birth.

A. O'Shaughnessy

The Descendants of the High Kings of Ireland, 1982–1998

I served as the President-General of the American Irish Historical Society for forty years. Each year, according to the bylaws of the Society, I delivered an Annual Address. The Society, and my ethnicity, have been important factors in the life of my family.

In Sliabh Luachra, in the shadow of the Paps of Dana, along the Kerry/ Cork border, there are hills and vales of great beauty and many small, poor farms. From these remote hills came the great Gaelic poets Egan O'Rahilly and Owen Roe O'Sullivan. A harsher reality can be found in local statistics documenting extreme levels of starvation during the Great Famine and emigration for the next fifty years. From Rathmore and Gneeveguilla, Knocknagree and Auniskirtane they trekked to Queenstown and began the long journey to America. That was the tale of my grandfather, and we were taught that "boat" relatives were sometimes even closer than "blood" relatives.

When I was a young boy, my father filled the house with tales of Irish heroes. Since the Cahills are direct descendants of the High Kings of Ireland, there was, naturally enough, a modest emphasis on our own genetic strain. In all fairness, I should note that the land of our forebears was blessed with an inordinate number of High Kings; the rest of the population were saints, scholars, poets, and patriots, although there was constant argument as to who belonged in the latter group.

After a series of reverses, the Court of the Cahill royal line moved from some misty mound in Ireland to a picturesque area just off Fordham Road in the Bronx. There, in coldwater apartments, affectionately known as the Kerry flats, were the heroes we were taught to admire. There was nothing mythical about them; they were Irish immigrants.

I could never quite distinguish between the blood relatives and the boat relatives, those who had shared the common bond of surviving together the trail to Ellis Island. To a youngster, these heroes were almost overwhelming; they certainly, on occasion, drank too much and fought mostly with words – and struggled, usually unsuccessfully, to shed the past too quickly. But far more impressive was how deeply they loved the clan, and they were loyal almost to a fault.

There was nothing subtle about their dreams. They had come to this land so that their children could enjoy a better life. These American Irish heroes did not leave the soft, gentle Ireland celebrated in song. The wealthy land owner and the city gentleman did not leave. Our ancestors were the survivors of oppression and famine, those desperate enough to seek refuge in steerage. But when their spirit burst forth upon this great land of the United States, they and the nation prospered.

They gave a strength to America that still nourishes her. The broad backs of the Irish laborers opened this nation's frontiers, built her railroads, dug her tunnels, and policed her streets. They were hod carriers and longshoremen, plumbers, painters, domestic servants, cooks and nannies and, soon enough, politicians, lawyers and doctors. With few publicized exceptions, the journey from poverty to security was not linked with lace curtains but with hard work, humor, a deep faith, and an almost unreasonable optimism in the future of the United States.

Eighty-five years ago a group of immigrant realists gathered, unheralded, in a cold Boston hotel room, and dreamed, not of the ancient past, but of a better future—for America and Ireland—and they began the tradition that we experience once again this evening. Out of steerage and fear and poverty, they determined that the Annual Meeting of their new American Irish Historical Society should be held at a banquet, much like the pilgrims celebrated their arrival in America—and their survival in a strange new land—with a feast on Thanksgiving. So, if we are able to dine tonight on five gourmet courses, we do so as the descendants of those who taught us to share our bounty and enjoy—with food and drink—the land that is ours.

A long, long time ago—and a very good time it was—when the world was much younger and more innocent, the land of our forebears was the playground of the likes of Angus Og, the God of love, who always had four bright birds hovering over his head in the form of kisses taking flight. There was brave Cuchulainn and Finn McCool, the Sons of Turenn and the Children of Lir, Grainne and Maev, Fergus mac Leda and the Wee Folk. Those who gather here tonight, whether they realize it or not, are made from those myths. For I suggest that what occurred in the remote ages has molded our characters and shaped the uniqueness of our ethnicity and our history.

The present is the child of the past and the seed of the future. As a historical society, we believe that appreciating and studying our heritage allows us to understand the fears and demons, hunger and anger, vulnerable beauty and the dreams—oh, most importantly the dreams—of those immigrant American Irish ancestors we represent here tonight.

Out of the ancient myths, sad odes, and doleful dirges somehow the American Irish discovered a foundation that did not bend with the temptations of a wider world. The dreams of those immigrants are an essential part of all of us and offer a perspective that the non Irish rarely understand, except on nights such as this when we assimilate all into our family, where everyone becomes, in some miraculous way, a brother, a sister, parent or child of each other. It is obviously difficult for the American Irish, especially when the romance of unity permeates a room, to distinguish dreams from reality.

We probably suspected, as children, that our ties to those ancestral kings of Ireland were exaggerated; nevertheless, the family legends put in perspective the significance of mere material goods and the transient, artificial power of titles and position. The lessons of a hard past, never forgotten, were softened by love and lore, and then passed on as tender buds of eternal hope for all who can still dream.

Yes, we have known loneliness and coldness and rejection, and those scars are just beneath the surface of most of us. The genes of our immigrant ancestors have left us a sensitive lot, easily moved to joy and sadness, maybe too easily hurt—too often by our own—but with a resiliency that permits us to overcome almost any obstacle, or at least adapt it to our own ends.

Part Two: Academia

A significant p⸜⸝ion of my adult life has been spent in academia. Research and teaching have been an integral part of my medical career, but, as will be clear from the speeches and essays selected for this section, I do not accept a restrictive definition for my profession. Institutions of higher education, including medical schools and teaching hospitals, should provide a civil setting for dialogue and investigation of, especially, competing ideas and ideologies.
The search for wisdom and understanding can flourish in the open and tolerant atmosphere expected of a university. This requires probing questions, honest debates, and challenges to sometimes almost universally accepted positions.
Over the past decades I have given dozens of university commencement addresses and probably hundreds of speeches about public policy in medical centers and other institutions of higher learning. My approach to most such talks was to seek an historical foundation, offer a global perspective, even for tragedies such as occurred on September 11th, and pose provocative questions to stimulate thought and discussion.

The Irish poet William Butler Yeats once described the tool he used in battle: "But weigh this song with the great and their pride / I made it out of a mouthful of air, / Their children's children shall say they have lied." *To persuade and educate a hostile or, even worse, an uninterested audience requires knowledge and logic and, if possible, humor. I have enjoyed the intellectual stimulation that flourishes in academic debate and have learned more than I have taught in the probing questions posed by students. The lecture theater is, for me, an extension of fieldwork in the tropics; the dress code may be different, and usually less comfortable, but the same passion and discipline are required to deliver a coherent message in a defined time.*

New Realities, New Frontiers
New York State Journal of Medicine, 1977

It was not too many years ago that I sat at just such a graduation, here at my alma mater, eager for the ceremony to be over, eager to shed the student's shackles. I left this great university and hospital complex with a healthy trepidation for the future and a sailor's respect for those sudden gusts of wind that so often alter the expected course of our lives. Although there were the normal fears of an undergraduate about to assume the responsibilities of a physician, I recall leaving Cornell Medical College more with a sense of wonder and expectation, an almost irrepressible sense of joy about the unknown paths ahead, and with an innocence that fostered dreams.

There were almost no boundaries that I saw, and my concept of medicine was broad enough to embrace the whole world and all its facets. As I did not have the knowledge of where my dreams and aspirations would take me, I hope that you too do not have rigid restrictions to your definition of medicine but are willing to go where your dreams lead, for those are, and always have been, the frontiers of our profession. Where those dreams lead are the borders beyond which physicians must learn to go, not only in the technical science of health but in the arts of sociology, politics, diplomacy, and, indeed, in all the humane endeavors that may make us a civilized people. Medicine is that rare field that can embrace all dreams and accommodate all aspirations.

My Bronx and Irish background must have provided a resiliency that not only sustained me through the poverty of student days, but also gave me the strength to embark from the harbor of academia on travels that, to say the least, were only partially mapped. I proudly acknowledge those Celtic traits that came from my physician—father—a willingness to seek the poetry of a good battle and to almost relish a fight against wrongs, no matter what the odds.

It has been said of the Irish that all their wars are merry, and all their songs are sad. If one did not approach this graduation with an historic and philosophic perspective, it might be very difficult indeed to find causes for merriment in the field of health for those about to begin their own journey of dreams today. For health care is in the throes of upheaval. Some of our hospitals are in bankruptcy; obscenely expensive malpractice premiums are common; physicians' incomes are publicized on the front pages of our newspapers; and Medicaid mills, brain death, and the right to die with dignity have become part of the semantics of medicine.

But I did not accept this gracious invitation to be your commencement speaker to detail the present plight of New York, or to identify the major crises in our health system, or to regale you with tales of how the current administration has met some of those challenges. I come before you not to utter a few polite meaningless words, but rather to encourage you and to share with you my dreams as well as my perception of reality.

It is almost embarrassing at times, when learning from colleagues of the troubles in our profession to realize how happy I have been in medicine. A fellow traveler in the desolate swamps of the Sudan, where I once worked for months, said he had the unreasonable feeling that he had found what he was searching for without ever discovering what it was.

The philosophy with which you enter the profession will determine whether you find opportunity in adversity or devour yourselves in bitterness and frustration at the inevitable and unknown changes to come. If, as a recent commencement speaker here contended, the goal of medical education is to produce members of a professional guild, then there may well be a valid basis for depression. While the traditions and ideals and goals of medicine may remain the same as in the days of Hippocrates, it would he self-deceptive to view the health system, or any of the health professions, in terms that might have been valid when Sir William Osler flourished a half century ago, or even when I graduated only sixteen years ago.

We cannot, we dare not, think in terms of yesterday's categories, but rather must work within the context, of today's realities, the new cultural, political, social, and economic forces that determine our actions. They are not evil any more than the patterns of the past were necessarily good. But, they are reality, and merely fighting these factors, rather than fashioning them to suit the present, is the sad recourse of futile and fatuous followers of a great profession that cries out for leaders. Leaders must emerge from your ranks, leaders who can demonstrate the ability, and often the agility, to preserve honor and heritage while adapting to the changing needs of society.

At the dedication of Johns Hopkins Medical School, almost a century ago, the great educator, Daniel Coit Gilman, noted that a university "misses its aim if she produces learned pedants, or simple artisans, or cunning sophists, or pretentious practitioners. Its purpose is not so much to impart knowledge as to whet the appetite. It should prepare, for the service of society, a class of students who will be thoughtful and progressive guides in whatever department of work or thought they may be engaged."

We should not expect the graduates who leave today to be trained in every technique, certainly not to be accomplished in the great art of patient care, but we can hope you have the capacity to grow, the flexibility to adapt, and the humility to deal with reality so you do not become prisoners of a profession. Medicine and nursing are like threads in the tapestry of society; as part of a pattern they have a golden splendor amid so many dull occupations and pursuits of man, but isolated from the flow of human events even these strands lose their luster and force.

I have had a rather unique opportunity to view the role of medicine in the realms of government, first at the international level, and in recent years, with responsibilities at a state level. Most of the challenges and opportunities that have come my way were not considered in the curriculum of the medical school, but were, thank God, found in the broad bases of this university's philosophy and in the Jesuit training in Thomistic logic that was part of the maturation process of all good Irish Catholics a generation ago.

The concepts, for example, that medicine could be wed with diplomacy to the benefit of both disciplines, that disease knows no national boundaries, and that the healing arts could provide the mortar that will eventually bind the wounds of a troubled world were theses I first propounded in a book entitled, *The Untapped Resource: Medicine and Diplomacy*. Only after a friend pointed out that, while it's nice to write a book, it is much more important to pass a law, did I become involved in a major move to alter the ways that this nation delivers health services abroad. We have worked for over ten years in this arena, knowing some victories and many defeats.

In the healing process lies the greatest potential to show humane love and by so doing confound the voices of hate throughout the world. That premise is critical as we seek the essential common ground from which one must address the division of people and the destruction of societies, whether that be in the Middle East, where I happily lived for a number of years, Northern Ireland, East Harlem, or throughout New York State.

We in medicine have an obligation to promote our approach to, and our understanding of, society's problems, as we must learn how to better utilize the talents and techniques of other professions. The Iroquois called the Hudson "the river that flows both ways," and so it is with medicine and society. Increasingly we recognize that the attack on disease is multidisciplinary. We do not hesitate to involve the engineer, the computer scientist, the anthropologist, or the sociologist. Is it timidity or indifference that prevents the physician and nurse from contributing their concepts and methods to the political process and its attack on complex public problems?

In New York State, where health care is a 15 billion dollar enterprise and public monies account for 42 percent of all funds spent in this field, we have been faced with a collision course in recent years. The state has had to make many hard choices, not only in regard to those programs directly funded by government but also in those which represent a de facto tax on our economically hard pressed citizens. Bold but necessary and often distasteful measures have restored the traditional fiscal integrity of the Empire State. This stability has been brought about, but not without a cost: to the poor; to the old; to the providers of human services in every area; and, of course, to all the people of the state who, in a variety of ways, have undertaken economies in their daily lives as they have also modified their expectations.

These decisions in health were made within a political context. Whether that was appropriate is not the question; it was reality, and therein lies the answer. No serious or responsible elected official could abdicate his responsibility for the vast budgetary and social implications of the health system. The role that those in the health field can assume in such a milieu is dependent on their ability to adapt their dreams to reality while offering the hope, the helping hand, and the wisdom that have been identified with the healing arts since time immemorial.

The physician has a privileged position from which to view the world, but alone he is almost impotent to effect any change. For too long medical professionals have spoken only to one another, documenting the toll of diseases, studying its causes and victims and calling on anyone and everyone to listen to their advice. They have failed, however, to move beyond the traditional limitations of the profession and to realize that merely convincing – or is it conversing with? – one another has neither altered economic policies nor significantly influenced political will; it is in these arenas that the critical decisions which determine the extent or even existence of health programs are made most frequently. Too rarely have competent, respected health experts been willing to venture from their safe havens into the turbulent councils where government priorities are established and financial allocations are set. Those best qualified have made too small a contribution to these councils in regard to the human resource, the human potential, and the impact of programs on people.

If there has been a sense of outrage at the human condition in many parts of the world, those who should be most able to express this have been either unable or unwilling to articulate the harsh realities of life as they exist for the majority of mankind. For too long, we who deal with and know most intimately the one unique resource, the human being, have allowed our projects to remain dreams and our priorities to be words.

Somebody, surely, will shape the future for good or for ill. If professionals in science and health continue to merely rail against the system and arrogantly absent themselves from the political process, they shall not have, and do not deserve, the power to fashion our society.

As you go forth today, I pray, with your family, teachers, and friends, that your dreams and aspirations may be realized. I hope for your own sakes, as well as for the professions of medicine and nursing, that you will have the courage to follow those dreams beyond the limits of your expectations. When you arrive at those new horizons and find reality, use the approach of the Irish poet, Yeats, who told his beloved:

"I have spread my dreams under your feet:
Tread softly because you tread on my dreams."

May you all find as much joy in that challenging interface of dreams and reality as has your grateful and honored commencement speaker.

The Peculiar Élan
1975 – 1981

This address was modified for scores of different universities and hospitals, but the principles which guided my actions during my six-year tenure in charge of health and mental health in New York State and my words remained much the same in different locations.

In the long haul of life, it is the philosophy – in this instance of an administration – that may make it memorable. The details of specific bills or the relentless activities of a bureaucracy are easily forgotten. It is so easy to lose the peculiar élan of an era and let sheer size – whether it be in business or academia or government – crush the individual flair and approach. It is so safe to be faceless and to treat constituents – or patients – as ciphers in a computer, divorcing the numbers from humans and living in that clean world where fear and failure, frustration and pain, bigotry and ugliness do not intrude. The job at hand may get done – it usually does some way or other – but as Eugene O'Neill said, "you can take the life out of the booze." Today, there is plenty of life in New York and a humane approach too long missing from the governmental scene.

There are ethical judgments that can no longer be avoided, and which, in fact, seem to distinguish our present dilemmas from the mundane. Preserving the protection of the court and the right to redress in a medical world obsessed with rising malpractice rates; the religious concerns about the definition of death, right to life, living wills, or DNA research; the balancing of community desires for stability with the right of the mentally disabled to be served in the least restrictive setting; the insanity defense and the death penalty – all are issues that touch upon the health of a society and clearly require major value judgments.

The critical decisions that guide our society must be made, not with an eye on the latest popularity poll but with the security of an age old ethic, not with arrogance but with love and compassion, not in selfishness but with generosity, and, God willing, with wisdom. In making those decisions we must resist the enormous temptation to let the system become the master and to believe that truth lies in a label. This fallacy occurs in medicine as well as in government, and too often the actions of society flow not from its values or convictions but reflect merely the weight of custom and inertia, of form and not substance.

One of the fundamental tenets of this administration's health policy is the firm, unshakeable conviction that, while we will do everything in our power to foster cooperation among the diverse elements of the health community, government itself must assume the role of leadership in bringing order and rationality and effective functioning to a chaotic, unrestrained, and fragmented system whose viability is essential for society. Only the state can effectively mobilize the multiple elements in the health care system to guarantee accessible, appropriate services at a price we can afford.

Certainly the cost of health care cannot be equated with human lives, pain, or suffering. Dollars are not equal in any proper balance of society with quality of care, accessibility of service, and excellence of medical manpower. Nevertheless, failure to contain – or even consider – costs in our health system over many decades was a major contributing cause that brought our state and its cities, towns, and counties to the verge of insolvency. New York City was not the only area dragged to the edge by crushing Medicaid and other runaway health related costs.

With the very lives of citizens at stake, the normal checks and balances of society not in play, the health system in disorder and the cost of medical services soaring out of reach, government had to assure reasonable access to such services and to regulate their quality, quantity, and cost. There is no need to apologize for active government involvement. It would have been utterly irresponsible to return to the passive role of the past.

Although the state's direct involvement in costs and access is relatively new, ample precedent is found in the state's constitutionally mandated public health role. There is scarcely a single act performed by any physician, or a procedure carried out in any hospital, that is not influenced in some measure by the actions of the state. Tests performed on the infant at the moment of birth are mandated by the state, as are procedures that are carried out at the pronouncement of death. Meeting that responsibility has been a challenge, made easier by the extraordinary numbers of concerned and committed citizens who have joined us. Their help has been needed for these have been very difficult days. There is neither glory, nor honor, nor praise for many of the decisions that must be made. There is no pleasure in defining who will do without.

A number of fundamental principles have guided our endeavors. First, we were determined to view the broad health of our people and not merely their medical needs. Second, I accepted my position on the premise that politics be removed from the health and mental hygiene systems, and my only mandate was to seek the most qualified for the many positions of service that needed to be filled.

Third, we opted for the most open approach possible and sought help wherever we could find it. We have formed new councils and many of the members have had the satisfaction of having their ideas translated into bills and signed into law. Last year, of the twenty two bills introduced as the "Governor's Health Program," twenty one were enacted by both the Senate and the Assembly and signed into law – a new and praiseworthy record. Lawmakers of both major parties recognized the state's health needs as far more important than partisan posturing. This bipartisan and open approach is essential if we are to deal effectively with the unrecognized giant of our economy, health care.

No wonder that changes were difficult to accomplish and, as retrenchment became the order of the day, that crises in the health industry seemed endless. There were no historical precedents for what had to be done, no textbook cases to use as guidelines. We knew we sometimes had insufficient data on which to make scientifically based decisions, but we couldn't afford to take the time for elaborate studies to protect our flanks or justify what commonsense demanded. We had to decide quickly and act immediately. Labor disputes and strikes broke out in hospitals and nursing homes, and the state, which had been for too long the passive onlooker that ultimately paid the freight, had to take a more active role in negotiations. The era of laissez-faire in health care was over, and all the elements had to adjust to a real world with finite resources.

Physicians and nurses differed over the very definition of their functions and over the growing use of physicians' assistants. Dissatisfied patients filed malpractice suits against doctors and hospitals, and premiums soared to the skies. Overcharging and other fraudulent practices involving Medicaid reimbursement were disturbingly commonplace. There were numerous findings of callous treatment of patients in some nursing homes and of misuse and diversion of funds.

Today, we still have our share of problems, but the malpractice rate escalation has abated. The fraudulent have been jailed, and landmark nursing home legislation enacted; there has been a rational reduction in the costly oversupply of acute care facilities with over thirty unnecessary hospitals and seven thousand health care beds closed, a record unequaled anywhere in the nation. The vast departments of health and mental hygiene – for many decades seemingly impervious to reform and immutable in the face of attempts to improve their functioning – were restructured to meet the challenging demands of society. Financing health care, controlling toxic chemicals, assuring community care for the retarded – these and many other issues required a radically revised organizational structure if the government bureaucracy was to become capable of responding to the dreams of its citizens. Organization not only reflects but can actually make policy, and these changes were essential if any progress was to be realized. Such changes have been accomplished not with an ax but with a scalpel, in as careful a way as possible.

In 1977, total Medicaid costs in New York State went down. This marked the first time that the Medicaid budget had fallen in any state since the inception of the national program back in 1967. Those of you who want to take a more careful look at the record, as Governor Al Smith was fond of saying, will find it in my book, *Health in New York State*. With the characteristic modesty of an author, I believe that book provides an accurate overview of the state's health problems, accomplishments, and potential.

In 1928, Franklin Delano Roosevelt stated, "The test of our progress is not whether we add more to the abundance of those who have much, it is whether we provide enough for those who have too little." By those standards this administration has tried to serve its citizens particularly in these times of retrenchment, when it is usually the least able who suffer the most. A fundamental – if unlikely – document to study when one is judging the values of an administration is the executive budget. Here, the political promises finally fade and, particularly in an era of limited resources, society's value judgments are translated into specific allocations.

In this administration, the only departments to be continuously expanded have been those of health, mental hygiene and corrections. For lip service will not sustain the poor, the needy, the prisoner, the vulnerable, and the disturbed, not to mention the sick. Our perception of humanism is in the record.

The University and Revolution
America, 1987

Universities reflect the societies they serve. At all times, universities try to teach the young to learn and to accept the burden of leadership; they prepare a new generation to take the torch of responsibility and educate those who must expand society's vision while preserving its traditions. In times of political stability, the university, the repository of historical and cultural wisdom, becomes the focus for the refinement of all that makes a civilization. During times of national debate, as in the United States during the Vietnam War, the university can become the center for dissent, coalescing the philosophic concerns of elders with the rebellious resistance of youth. During times of revolution, a university, particularly a Catholic and Jesuit university, must fill all these roles and do even more – it must somehow capture the dreams of the liberated, translate the soul of the struggle, and define for a skeptical world the goals of rebellion.

There is nothing terribly new in this mandate. Cardinal John Henry Newman, in his *Idea of a University,* summarized these aims a century ago: "A university training is the great ordinary means to a great but ordinary end; it aims at raising the intellectual tone of society, at cultivating the public mind, at purifying the national taste, at supplying true principles to popular enthusiasm and fixed aims to popular aspiration, at giving enlargement and sobriety to the ideas of the age, at facilitating the exercise of political power..."

Cardinal Newman's noble goals were not conceived in worldly security. They were delivered in nineteenth century Dublin, where bigotry, discrimination, and economic exploitation denied Irish Catholics access to academia. They reflected the revolutionary dreams of the poor; they were a cry for decency and dignity, a demand for quality and equality. If they were born in isolation and rejection, they have, nonetheless, grown into the universal ideals of higher education.

It is important to recall the humble origins of Cardinal Newman's idea, for it may serve a Latin America in need of courage. As Julio Cortázar, an Argentinean poet and novelist, has so beautifully noted, "The reality of Latin America... is almost always agitated and tormented. There are situations of oppression and shame, of injustice and cruelty, of the submission of entire peoples to relentless forces bent upon maintaining them in a state of illiteracy.... It is on this field, stained with blood, torture, imprisonment, and degrading demagoguery, that literature – and universities – wage battles, as on others they are waged by visionary politicians and activists who often give their lives for a cause that may seem utopian to many, but is not."

It is within the great tradition of Newman and the passionate counsel of Julio Cortázar, that the University of Central America (UCA) has assumed such a prominent place in the intellectual life of Nicaragua today. This independent seat of learning has opted for social involvement as its method of perfecting the revolution and has made its resources available for the development of the nation; it fashions the response of an educated urban elite to the problems of slum dwellers and campesinos.

There can be no barriers at the campus gates for a university in a revolution. If the special needs of the poor and social justice for all are the goals of a revolution, then a university must consider these aspirations or wither away in irrelevancy. Entrusted with the minds and imaginations of the young, a university cannot survive as an island; training students in social action projects is as legitimate a part of a first rate education as is teaching them the classics.

Robert Kennedy once noted that the future is not a gift, but an achievement that has to be earned, that the future does not belong to those who are content with today, but neither does it belong to those who are content to forget the past. Linking the academic curriculum and professional staff of a university with the needs of a community in revolution promotes current progress while preserving traditional values. Ideally, the university should be able to reach these dual goals unfettered. Some six hundred years ago, St. Thomas Aquinas and the Teachers' Guild in Paris (all of whose members were clerics) developed the concept of the university, or studium, as a third force that has a necessary independence from the civil authority, or regnum, and the ecclesiastical authority or sacerdotium. In a revolution, the university cannot afford to be divorced from the struggle, but it also cannot allow itself to become the handmaiden of a political party or particular ideology. The university must be free in its search for truth and in its ability to analyze events constructively and to criticize theories effectively.

The very nature of a university rebels against the imposition of either secular or religious orthodoxy. In preserving its essential independence, the university protects the fundamental goals of a revolution, those fragile dreams of freedom that must be nourished by debate or die. With concentrated wisdom and understanding it can emerge as the true alma mater, assisting in the formation of a conscience for the nation, guiding the leaders of the present and molding the minds of future generations.

This is not an easy task. Your rector Cesar Jerez, S.J., in an acclaimed Notre Dame address last year, expressed the challenge of the UCA in trying to reach those who have "become numb through suffering, silent through fear, skeptical through disillusion, or so absorbed by the daily task of survival as to be incapable of other preoccupations." Yet, if freedom and liberty are to be realized, an educated citizenry is more essential to an ongoing revolution than weapons. Both partners in a marriage make commitments, and while the university can assist government with social projects, the state must manifest its belief in education by example and support.

One of the most remarkable demonstrations of the critical importance of a university to a revolution is the current effort of President Daniel Ortega to continue his law studies. Having abandoned his formal education in 1965 to participate in an armed struggle for independence, he has now returned to complete the academic demands of the legal profession and, in doing so, he offers a unique lesson to his country. Neither the military nor the presidency confer degrees; a university establishes standards in education, and even the most powerful must seek its recognition. That lesson of mutual respect and cooperation is being watched around the world.

What the Superior General of the Society of Jesus Peter-Hans Kolvenback, S.J. said in a sermon he gave in Caracas, Venezuela, on October 12, 1984, can surely be applied to the work of UCA: "It is Latin America that has opened the eyes of all Jesuits to the preferential love for the poor and to the fact that the true, integral liberation of men and women must take priority as the focus of the mission of the Society of Jesus today." As so often happens in history, Jesuit educators are once again on that borderline where the church meets the world. The business of a university is knowledge. Sharing that knowledge with a nation striving toward the basic rights of literacy and health will guarantee UCA a place of pride when the history of the revolution can ultimately be written. May that day of peace come soon.

The Symbolism of Salamanca
University of Nicaragua Press, 1990

After the Sandinista government had been overthrown, and the goals of the revolution crushed, I gave this talk at a Convocation at the National Autonomous University of Nicaragua, 1990.

Several years ago, in an address at your neighboring college here in Managua (The University of Central America, 1987), I suggested that "a university reflects the society it serves," that if academia was to thrive in the throes of a revolution it must assert its relevance by crossing the campus gates, temporarily forsaking the privileged protection of lecture halls and immersing itself in the struggles of the oppressed.

Time has passed, taking its toll on the dreams of those who envisioned a new society in Central America. The will of an exhausted people has apparently sought refuge in the relative safety of past practices and postures, accepting, at least for the present, the realities and traditional exercise of power in this hemisphere. The slogans are now muted, the focus of world attention is elsewhere, and the tensions of a decade seem to have faded into columns of sterile statistics documenting a return to the predictable supplicant position of a small, dependent country.

What is the role of a national university at this point in your history? What constitutes the society it is supposed to reflect, and whom does it serve? There are precedents that offer both direction and courage in answering these questions, and in facing existing and future challenges.

As Salamanca fell to the Falangist forces of Franco and his superpower allies of the day, the great Spanish philosopher, Miguel de Unamuno, served as rector of the local university. In his last Convocation, just weeks before he died, he faced a hostile audience of government officials who resented academic autonomy and the risks inherent in unfettered intellectual research, thought and expression. They scorned the old man, crying "Muerte a la inteligencia" – death to the intellectuals.

He waited in vain for quiet and then slowly responded, "*Venceréis, pero no convenceréis...* – You will win, but you will not convince. You will win because you possess more than enough brute force, but you will not convince since to convince means to persuade. And in order to persuade you would need what you lack, reason and right in the struggle. I consider it futile to exhort you to think of Spain. I have finished." And he was led away by a one eyed general whose name and transient power are now forgotten. But the thoughts of Unamuno still inspire scholars around the world, and his philosophy of the tragic sense of life is debated wherever free men gather. His beloved University of Salamanca continues its influence far beyond the parochial confines of small town Spain.

Modern day Managua might well remember the example of Unamuno and the symbolism of Salamanca. At the nadir of Spanish fortunes, that nation found solace in her intellectual leaders. The university drew on its rich past while analyzing the frenetic and destructive present. Scholars tried to unravel the causes of national suicide while artists distilled conflicts into painting, poetry, and philosophy. The university became a center for healing, for civilized dialogue, for gradual reconciliation.

Seeds, planted in a new generation of students, flourished in an atmosphere where challenges and criticism were recognized as essential elements of education and not condemned merely because they differed from popular positions. The students grew in an environment where the barriers of class structure steadily fell before the impartial power of open debate.

Unamuno insisted that those who could lead a life of the intellect must come to know the pain of poverty in their communities. He then urged them to employ every tool available to foment disaffection among a placid populace who, he believed, did not rebel largely because they had never been taught to think of other options or to realize that suffering and failure need be neither perpetual nor inevitable.

The inherent freedom of a university allows the escape valves of irony and satire, exposing political pandering and pomposity, the clichés of expediency and oppression. Such freedoms, universally recognized as essential for intellectual survival, can be, as you well know, dangerous, for their exercise too often attracts reprisals from the powerful and insecure. Attempts to control freedom of expression within a university will always ultimately fail, and it is important, at convocations such as this, to recall but a few of the inalienable rights, ancient roles, and glorious possibilities you possess. For example, academia can:

1. *Preserve the heritage* and national pride of a people.

2. *Protect scholars* and their freedom to investigate and disseminate their findings.

3. *Promote a better future* for all by expanding qualified teaching throughout the country. In meeting this challenge, it would be well for a national university to sensitize students by promoting a preferential option for research on the problems of the poor. Students, early in their careers, would then have the experience, and, one hopes, the satisfaction, of working with their mentors on the unresolved ills of a battered society. Involvement in, and concern for, such problems, would lead to a greater mutual respect between "town" and "gown," producing *compañeros* striving, each with their own talents and instruments, to

establish a unified nation. The uneducated, instead of resenting universities as isolated and exclusive pockets of elitism, could learn, by absorption, how to break the bonds of ignorance that now cripple their mental and emotional, as well as physical, lives.

4. *Develop a unique service* to government, the private sector, and even religious organizations. Each of these groups, by its very nature, is forced to deal with daily demands for service or profits. They are rarely able to undertake the research necessary to create new models for critical social, economic, agricultural, and medical projects. In devising innovative solutions to old problems, only the university can offer an unbiased, independent approach that, combined with a concentration of skills and talent, makes her a full and equal partner in the common weal.

5. *Help redefine and reinterpret* the terms and meanings of new government regulations that alter almost every aspect of the daily lives of your fellow citizens.

Only the academy has the necessary credibility and legitimacy for this task, especially at times of revolutionary change. I have worked in Nicaragua for over twenty years, with radically different regimes in power. My sympathy for the goals of the Sandinistas is well known to this audience; your high honor to me at this convocation demonstrates, I would like to think, that continuity of service and love binds us together in the endless struggle of Unamuno – to affirm the nobility of the intellect and the importance of the university in the evolving life of a nation. The ancient academic traditions of Salamanca will serve you well in the difficult transition period you now face.

The scope of all great calamities are ultimately reflected in cold statistical charts of individual deaths. To those who experience personal loss, the impact of conflict or natural disaster can be terrible indeed. But to have any valid understanding, one must measure tragedy in mortality numbers. Millions of innocent women and children have died from disease and starvation over the past four decades in Somalia and Sudan, and I saw much of this; almost a million were hacked to death in a single month in Rwanda as the world stood by. The list in our lifetime could go on and on, from Armenia to Srebrenica, from the Congo to Central America. This was an important, if difficult, perspective to remind Americans

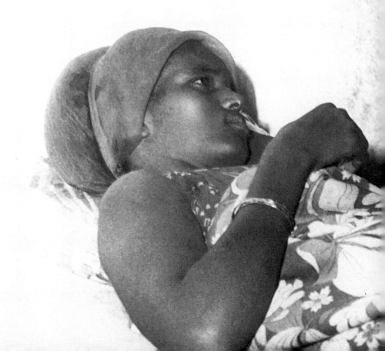

of as they tried to cope with the terrorist assaults that killed a bit under 3,000 people on September 11th, 2001. Shortly thereafter, I was appointed the Chief Medical Advisor for Counterterrorism to the New York Police Department. I believe it is important to keep a balance if we are to live in an international world that also knows the constant fear of death and the reality of tragedy. The Somali woman in this picture was facing imminent death from a prolonged obstructed childbirth hundreds of miles from any adequate medical care. I am examining her on the dirt floor of a clinic where she was resting after I had performed an emergency Caesarian section the night before. Mother and baby survived.

Grief and Renewal
UN Chronicle, 2001

It is a privilege to be asked to share in this memorial service at Pace University but also, and just as important, to be present at your time of renewal. These emotions – grief, approaching despair, and overwhelming, abiding hope are not contradictory or mutually exclusive. Particularly for the young, hope for a better future is a fundamental part of your being. It is why you study at a university. To learn, to expand your minds so that you can contribute to others, and maybe, just maybe, make a saner world for your children and their children.

Today, it is both your solidarity with the dead and the injured, combined with your determination and commitment to begin a new era, that offer the finest tribute to the memory of those we honor. To you who have lost loved ones and to you who are physically or mentally scarred by this trauma, do not be afraid; do not underestimate your capacity to heal and to grow. You can, and you simply must, go on, and we all must learn from this disaster.

My own perspective on tragedy is somewhat unusual. Every day most physicians deal with human tragedy, since pain and death are integral parts of medical life. Usually these are individual events, and few physicians are prepared for enormous catastrophes. But for over forty years, I have worked in troubled parts of Africa, Asia, and Latin America. My perspective on human tragedy is tempered by such experiences and may offer a necessary balance as we Americans ponder the terrorist acts that destroyed the World Trade Center and part of the Pentagon, killed thousands of innocent people, and disrupted life around the world. Because I deal with epidemic diseases and the potentials of bioterrorism, I have been at the emergency command post and down at the Ground Zero site. No words – at least I do not have words – can describe the rubble there, with fused body parts strewn across a landscape we knew so well.

Since our American Civil War, almost one hundred and fifty years ago, we have been spared such scenes in the United States. Geography isolated us from recent conflicts. World War I and World War II passed our land by, but we must remember that the specter of death and destruction is well known in almost every other part of the world. We must not forget that London and Stalingrad, Dresden and Hiroshima, Dubrovnik and Grozny have all been almost obliterated and yet, with courage and hard work, with help from friends and former enemies, they came back to life as cities and societies. In our sorrow today, as we honor our thousands dead and missing, we must also remember that a million people were hacked to death a few years ago in Rwanda. I worked in Somalia when hundreds of thousands of innocent women and children starved to death. Every one of those dead had a father and mother, a sister or a brother, a child or a lover. Somehow keeping that perspective has always helped me to carry on, to try to help others to heal. I firmly believe we are all part of one world. We in America have been the most fortunate, and we have every right to defend our way of life. But we would indulge in an obscene and dangerous deception if we think this is the only tragedy to befall mankind.

Those are not, I hope, unfeeling words on a day when one rightly expects sympathy. But healing will take more than mere expressions of sympathy. It will begin—as your university proudly does every day—by mixing the wisdom and efforts of all cultures and races and religions in an endless struggle to find better ways to root out hatreds and end the cycles of violence, part of which exploded just two weeks ago right here, in your neighborhood, on September 11th.

America has demonstrated its heart in remarkable ways in the past fortnight. There are lines of good people donating their blood and their money and their time as volunteers. We've had a tireless mayor lead this city out of chaos and encourage life to return to normal. The solutions that America uses in responding to the terrible terrorist acts we have endured must reflect our resolve, and our power to punish and destroy those who tried to end our way of life. But as any physician knows, a surgical excision is but a tool in therapy. The first obligation is to define the root causes of a disease and know how it evolves before devising a rational treatment. Even in mental illness, one must try to understand the bases of disturbed thoughts if one is to penetrate those terrible dark areas of paranoia and hatred. I pray that our national response will be based on all the unique qualities that make America great. The world must see the heart of America, as we have seen it here in New York in the last few days.

This memorial service will end with the lighting of candles; the flame has long been a symbol of the search for knowledge and truth. You, in your university years, are the new generation that must carry on that search, and you now know that, here in New York, you are no longer alone. You have lived through an incredible period that binds us together. It is important that you go forth in confidence and in love, using the power of the mind and heart rather than the tools of revenge and violence. I wish you well in this difficult but essential endeavor.

To Bind our Wounds
Lenox Hill Hospital, New York, 9/11/2002

Throughout the centuries, those who survive disasters have offered memorials to the dead, and they have done so with different tools and different skills: Picasso did it for the victims of Guernica with oil paints. Verdi mourned the poet-patriot Manzoni with a musical masterpiece. Graveyards and public squares are full of sculpture and architecture dedicated to those we loved and those we honor as fallen heroes. Many of us, however, still record our losses and deepest sorrows with words. I've always been fascinated by words, by the challenge of trying to capture an essence in a well formed phrase, an image in the structure of a sentence, and then molding the flow of words so that ideas and coherent arguments emerge. There is something very satisfying—something almost inherently good—in identifying words, simple sounds with meaning, to link our most personal inner feeling with external facts and events. We create words that can withstand the pressures of reality and sustain us on our journeys of discovery into the private depths of our souls as well on our sometimes even more perilous excursions into contact with other human beings and nature itself.

I'm not sure that my memory of last September 11th and the weeks thereafter is as comprehensive as I would have liked in preparing this special memorial address. But I vividly recall the verbal reaction at the time—a moral certainty on the part of leaders summarized in words suitable for centers of religious worship, or "sound bites" for the current church of the masses, the evening television shows. They offered a global philosophy based on words from a simpler era—a "you're either with us or against us" view of the world. But wrapping oneself in a flag, or invoking God to justify aggression and preemptive strikes, seemed to me a rhetoric disconnected from the complex world I know, a world of diversity and rich but varying values and traditions that simply cannot be forced into a single mold.

A few months ago, when I was asked to deliver this talk, I thought how apt it would be to go back 138 years and quote from the Gettysburg Address. As all of you now know, that brief, beautiful memorial is being recited today by the Governor and the President, and, it seems, by every public official of every political party in every State of the Union. So I read further in Lincoln's biography and realized that for this September 11th anniversary program at Lenox Hill Hospital, it would be far more appropriate to cite a few lines from Lincoln's Second Inaugural Address. These provide the framework for my talk.

At his Second Inaugural, as the Civil War was grinding to a bloody close, President Lincoln used the words of medicine to help prepare a battered nation for a time of healing, of reconciliation, and reconstruction. The war had been pursued with firmness, and there were many who wanted to wreak vengeance on, and demand total submission from, the vanquished. Lincoln, however, urged his audience to "bind up the nation's wounds" and "to care for him who shall have borne the battle, and for his widow and his orphans."

That is our privileged role every day in medical life—to bind wounds, to care for the afflicted. Today, it is from this solid foundation that I suggest we must develop the courage to move beyond the traditional restraints of our profession. We must share our wisdom and experience for the sake of our nation, as it once again struggles in a search for a way out of a war mentality and towards a new era of peace.

We should also learn from Lincoln that the way forward cannot be based merely on violence against violence. In fact, if our society is ever to regain security and tranquility, there is no safe way forward based on vengeance and no possible way if we fail to see—and address—the wrongs that prompted our adversaries to their actions. In that Second Inaugural Address, at the end of a bitter and long conflict, wearily but wisely, President Lincoln said that the only way forward was "with malice towards none, and with charity towards all."

For almost a century and a half after Lincoln spoke these simple, profound words, our nation was spared the physical and psychological effects of an assault on our shores. Will we listen today to the wisdom of Lincoln, to the strong, but forgiving, caring, and gentle President, or will we attempt to memorialize our dead by assuring more dead in an endless cycle of violence? Health workers are among the most respected members in our society and we have, I believe, an opportunity – as well as an obligation – to rekindle Lincoln's spirit in a scarred nation in danger of being isolated in its own pain.

In this solemn memorial, we do not gather here today only as individuals or as citizens, but as members of the Lenox Hill Hospital family, with our own images of those tense days a year ago permanently seared in our minds. I am certain that most of you who work in this building can recall the almost surreal weeks that followed last September 11th. The streets around our hospital were filled with desperate people searching for their missing, with the walls and doors around the emergency room covered with photographs of the almost certainly dead. In the evening one could hear, as the crowds thinned, the silent cry of the anguished.

And then Lenox Hill Hospital became the scene of a fatal bioterrorist assault, with pulmonary anthrax snuffing out the life of one of our own family. Most of you can also recall the lines of frightened and confused employees waiting to receive their prophylactic antibiotic supply from the Department of Health. Although the initial cutaneous anthrax cases at NBC did not require inpatient care in our hospital, many of you know that I diagnosed those first two cases and was in close contact with our medical and laboratory colleagues. Our hospital, located in the very heart of New York, cared for one sixth of the entire national number of anthrax cases.

"Ground Zero" was not merely the dramatic rubble where the World Trade Center once stood. It was a newly vulnerable city. With anthrax, we discovered how fear could paralyze a society as efficiently as missiles. Anthrax, never previously seen by most physicians, was now a topic to be taught to interns and residents. Yet, as health workers must, every day of our lives, we learned and adapted.

In fact, I believe that medicine's age old tradition to learn from failure, to constantly adapt, to modify therapies in the daily battle with disease, offers a model for a way out of our current national morass. Medicine offers a unique way of looking at problems, a way that now seems almost absent in our country's political lexicon. The discipline of medicine reflects a capacity to see and study disaster, and not to waver, but to discover new approaches—even if progress must come in the autopsy room—and to think afresh, every day, on chronic, intractable, sometimes uniformly fatal diseases.

So today, as we all remember the destruction and deaths caused by terrorists, and some sadly reflect on their own personal losses, we must also use the occasion to recommit ourselves to applying the noble heritage of medicine to the ills of society. I believe there are fundamental contributions that the medical community can offer our nation today.

I began my own career in tropical medicine in the slums of Calcutta and first saw widespread starvation there. Later, I worked as a doctor in refugee camps in Somalia and the southern Sudan and lived with disease and death on a massive scale. I have been caught behind the lines in armed conflicts and seen senseless slaughter in Beirut and Managua and all across the scarred landscape of modern Africa. Somehow, in the twisted wreckage of war and in the squalor of refugee camps, the beauty of humanity prevailed for me.

Medicine and public health provide a common language, understood all over the world, and a philosophic approach that has sustained humanity's ageless search for healing without causing further damage, for respecting all wounded regardless of their affiliations or viewpoints, for creating calm and order from chaos, for promoting peace where there was war. The methodology of public health may provide a new and imaginative way to solve problems in the far less specific arenas of diplomacy and public policy. At the very least, such an approach offers a badly needed balance to the current national emphasis of trying to address our problems solely with overwhelming force. In his Nobel Prize acceptance speech, William Faulkner said the will of man is "not merely to endure but to prevail." But we need not prevail over someone else. Rather, we must learn to prevail with and through others. Only in that way will our society realize that growth and development can be achieved without destruction, and that we, in a field devoted to helping and healing, may hold the answer to a future based on mutual security and safety.

Wanton killing and brutality within supposedly sovereign borders, ethnic and religious strife, millions of starving or near starving refugees, other millions of migrants fleeing their homes out of fear for their lives or in a desperate search for a better life, human rights trampled down, appalling poverty in the shadows of extraordinary wealth, inhumanity on an incredible scale in what was supposed to be a peaceful dawn following the fall of the Berlin Wall: these are the awesome challenges that face us just as much as the hidden terrorists determined to destroy our way of life. The challenges are quite different from the nation-state rivalries and alliances that preoccupied statesmen during most of the past century. They call for earlier diagnoses and new kinds of therapy. Underlying causes have to be attacked sooner rather than later, before they become fulminating infections that rage beyond rational control or political containment.

Almost five hundred years ago, in a small book that remains a classic text, Machiavelli employed analogies with health in explaining a fundamental tenet of governance. He wrote:

When trouble is sensed well in advance, it can easily be remedied; if you wait for it to show, any medicine will be too late because the disease will have become incurable. As the doctors say of a wasting disease, to start with it is easy to cure but difficult to diagnose; after a time, unless it has been diagnosed and treated at the outset, it becomes easy to diagnose but difficult to cure. So it is in politics.

There are several important lessons in that quote. The shrewd and cynical Machiavelli knew that health images would help make his message clear to a skeptical public, and he wisely noted that politics is part of life. Most physicians have shied away from politics. We need not be ashamed of, and should not be hesitant to become involved in, political life. Our health profession has so much to offer that is rare in public life today. At its best, medicine, as a way of life, can provide some of those almost forgotten standards on which our fragile society must ultimately rely in its endless struggle for stability, prosperity, and peace.

Ancient principles guide the discipline of clinical medicine –qualities we take for granted such as confidentiality, discretion, honesty, integrity, respect for other's bodies and minds, whether those be beautiful or, in the eyes of the world, diseased and deformed. It is in the daily application of clinical medicine's unique mix of art and science that we win the respect and honor that is ours. And it is by using this stature and credibility that we can influence public policy above and beyond our own profession.

On this first anniversary of a terror filled day, it behooves us to remember the universality of tragedy and disaster, and also, very importantly, to recall the global outpouring of sympathy for America after September 11th. That brief shared identity, a spontaneous warm international reaction, a solidarity that money couldn't buy, it seems to me, holds something precious for the future. There is nothing shameful or weak in admitting our pain. It is a reality doctors and nurses deal with every day, one that allows patient and health worker to become one in the battle against illness. So, too, can a proud nation, wounded and hurt, grow stronger and better if we recognize in tragedy the chance for new foundations. If we do not grow from our pain, all will be wasted in an arrogant selfish isolation, fueled by the evil fear of other colors and religions.

Those who suffer, and are rejected, are the predictable perpetrators of future terrorist attacks, and no amount of counterintelligence or preemptive attacks will stamp out these huge populations. If health workers have the skills to heal individuals, as well as the tools to stop epidemics and even eliminate diseases from the face of the earth, then we should not – in fact we cannot – absent ourselves from this new war on terrorism, a war with no apparent end and few definable borders. New solutions are obviously needed, and they may lie, silently and unappreciated, in the rich traditions of our profession.

Many years ago, in the midst of a raging civil war in the southern Sudan, I participated in humanitarian actions which opened doors to negotiated settlements. Even in the midst of armed conflict, neutral and impartial immunization efforts for children were begun. These programs created corridors of understanding that led to de facto cease fire periods and, eventually, became permanent bridges to peace.

Since that time I have worked with humanitarian and diplomatic leaders around the world, and today there is a growing consensus that the failed approaches of the past will inevitably fail again. Power politics and military actions may provide transient solutions; but, to be lasting, these efforts must be coordinated with health and human rights and educational improvements. Health workers are, therefore, major partners if peace is to be realized, and we must assume new responsibilities in a world where another failure may prove to be the final act of civilization. In my book *Preventive Diplomacy*, the somewhat immodest subtitle is *Stopping Wars Before They Start*. But, for everyone's sake, that is what we must try.

In a small examining room in my medical office there is a painting of an American flag done by an Irish artist. Many years ago, the artist, sitting on the porch of our home and looking at our national flag, suddenly said "Do you not see the heart in the stars?" I share this image because it captures so much of what I feel today.

America demonstrated its heart in remarkable ways in the period after the September 11th attacks. We all know the stories of those who rescued the disabled and then went back into the burning World Trade Center buildings to save their fellow workers. We know of the heroic work of police and firefighters, and one had only to see, as I did, the people in the command center and down at the Ground Zero site to know that America has a very big heart indeed. We saw this spirit at Lenox Hill Hospital after the anthrax attacks.

America demonstrated a heart that we may have always known was there but, as is our fashion, was too rarely exposed. It is critically important today that the world understand that America is a nation of caring and compassion. If we are perceived as only a military power that will seek only vengeance, then violence and retribution will inevitably continue. For many years, I have been, as my wife sometimes suggests, obsessed with the idea that health and humanitarian affairs ought to be central in our foreign policy, not peripheral afterthoughts. We have failed, as a great nation, to let the outside world understand the goodness of our people, to be as proud of America's "heart in the stars" as we are of our undoubted strength.

Persisting in our current national responses to the attacks of last September 11th, responses that are predictable, and even understandable, but tragically limited, will assure a perpetuation of threats and violence against Americans everywhere. Is it not obvious that we must expand our options, create bold new initiatives that address all aspects of a complex crisis that is now endangering America's heart and soul as well as its physical body? We can, as Lyndon Johnson once said, walk and chew gum at the same time. An earlier president, Harry Truman, noted that he was good at making decisions when there were no alternatives. Choosing to continue reacting with only military might, abandoning the very foundations on which this great nation was built, indulging in gross violations of human rights and dignity for the illusion of safety is not—and should not—be an alternative. We have lived through an incredible year, one that has bound us together as never before. It is important that we go forth in confidence, and in love, using the power of the mind and the heart, and the mores of medicine, to secure a more united and safe America and a better world.

I have been honored by your invitation to speak at this memorial ceremony among my colleagues and friends. May God bless all of you, especially this hospital family, and may God bless America.

Loaded Words
Manhattanville College, 2003

A number of years ago, after I had accepted the invitation to give my first commencement address, I thought back to my own graduation, and, for the life of me, could not remember who the speaker was or what he had said. At first blush, I thought that this sort of academic amnesia might be peculiar to myself. But an informal poll that I conducted among friends assuaged my guilt. Very few of them—less than one percent, I would say—could recall a single phrase or thought from their baccalaureate addresses. In the face of such statistics, I must say it takes a lot of courage for a commencement committee to ask someone to join the ranks of the forgotten, and maybe only a fool, a dreamer or an inveterate optimist would accept.

Every wise commencement speaker also faces a definite

reality—how to uphold the ancient academic tradition of delivering a final message of inspiration while simultaneously respecting the schedules of the graduates and their families, friends, and admirers, who, very understandably, want only to be released so they can celebrate their great day of accomplishment. The reason, it seems to me, that one accepts an invitation to deliver a commencement address is that it offers an important opportunity to identify with you, to mark the common ground between those of us who have tried to accomplish something for their fellow man and a new generation that must carry on this endless struggle. A commencement speaker is not here for the dais dignitaries, the faculty, the trustees, or even the president. He or she comes to honor the graduates, those who have successfully completed their studies and are about to begin their own journeys.

We have used a lot of loaded words so far—completion, beginning, tradition, celebration, ceremony, and even inspiration. Do they fit? Do such words and phrases really help us face the joys as well as the inevitable sorrows ahead, the disappointment and the failures of life? I hope so, for, it would seem to me, higher education should liberate, and strengthen, not only the mind, but also the heart and soul. It is in these hidden and special areas that your training and experience should help you deal with the reality of maturity—where innocence is not lost but refined, where continuing curiosity replaces false confidence, where humility and modesty are recognized as far better tools than arrogance in dealing with success as well as sadness.

Education should have brought to you an appreciation of your own individual wonder and given you the courage to share, even if there are dangers in exposing your vulnerabilities. Without that courage nothing good happens—people wouldn't fall in love, they wouldn't sacrifice to make other lives better, they wouldn't grow, gently and generously, accepting other's faults as well as their virtues. There is a time to leave the nest, and it takes strength and courage to complete the evolution from dependent child supported by a loving family to the caring, compassionate, responsible adult who now must help guide and sustain those less fortunate, those who will need your help.

Your education here should have broadened your scope and made it more difficult to be wrapped in a cocoon of self-interest.

It should have forced your mind to travel beyond the confines of place, beyond the narrow interests of a particular profession to participate in man's unending struggle – past and present – for dignity and decency. And like travel, your education should have provided you with lessons in humility and understanding, in kindness and tolerance.

It should also have provided you with an intellect that can change as life changes because, almost ironically, it should be deeply rooted in tradition. These academic gowns represent the great heritage of learning institutions here and abroad. They represent a tradition of which you are now the heirs. I do not speak of tradition as something to be merely preserved and venerated. I speak of tradition as that wise mother who nourishes and instructs her children and, having brought them to the threshold of maturity, sends them off to find their own place in the world. She knows that their world, in so many ways, will be quite different from her own, but she knows, too, that she has given them the principles and values on which the important decisions in any life are based.

With these, we can make sense of the world; we can help direct the rushing current of events which we cannot stop; we can discern a pattern amid confusing multiplicity. Hopefully, you might do the job better than we have, trying to predict and avoid problems rather than cause or merely deal with them after they explode. I do not mean to advocate a simplistic view of life. I know as well, and maybe better than most, that certainty is a rare commodity in the larder of human understanding, and I doubt that your four years at university have provided you with very many ready answers.

The physician may have an obvious opportunity to help and heal, but all of you have this gift, this obligation, every day for the rest of your lives. Opportunities emerge in the private, as well as in the public, roles you will undertake – in the arts, the sciences, in business, in organizing labor unions, in the home, the factory, through the wondrous new fields of communication and the internet. You will not have instant gratification and there is no certain blueprint to guide your path. There is, however, the joy of the struggle and the satisfaction of the quest. It is also very clear, in our post September 11th America, that you may meet tragedy at the most unexpected time and place.

The temptation may be strong to remain quiet and avoid the fray, to seek security in anonymity, to believe that the individual can have little impact on the multiple systems that affect our lives. Each generation deludes itself by thinking that the demands imposed on it are more rigorous than what its predecessors had to bear, that the problems are more insoluble now than then, that it is suffering a complexity in human life never before encountered, that far more is expected of its members than was of those before them. And commencement speakers often encourage this delusion by sending their young listeners off with the charge to resolve the problems that their fathers created.

All of this somehow does not ring true to experience. It denies the continuity of human life. It is too naïve a view of the world. People have always needed to struggle. Right never triumphed spontaneously over wrong. Integrity has always been maintained only through acts of courage. Compassion has never been worth a damn unless it manifested itself in concrete acts of love.

Compassion and charity do not always prevail, and we may have to artificially create periods of tranquility in the throes of apparently intractable confrontations. International pressure and aid can usually be generated to support such efforts. But it is during these lulls that one can initiate the difficult process that may well begin in argument but can evolve into civilized dialogue and, eventually, allow those shared efforts that are indispensable in the reconstruction of a torn society. Such a path has great risks, but establishing a firm foundation for diplomacy out of the human tragedies and political failures of the past is an approach we must explore. There are very few options left.

Wisdom comes slowly, especially to those who live in societies where we take security for granted and are accustomed to praise. Just as it takes time and experience to change the romance of youth into love, so too is it true in public affairs. In the relationships between nations and neighboring ethnic groups it requires maturity and understanding to withstand those easy temptations of instant gratification in order to develop alliances that are lasting, harmonious, and encourage mutual growth.

A university education should have provided you with a strong foundation to analyze, and even understand, the frightening complexities of our modern world. Knowledge and training offer you the inordinate privilege of learning to help as well as to rule, of discovering the rewards that come with reaching out a healing hand to the vast majority of your brothers and sisters who suffer and die prematurely. No one has yet devised standardized methods or satisfactory vehicles to integrate the ideals and experiences of the university with the anger and frustration of the ignorant, oppressed, and ill masses of this world. But their dreams and demands are real, and they will not be stilled and cannot be crushed. For all our sakes—yours as well as theirs—you must learn to participate in the new and much needed diplomacy I have outlined, one that I believe offers the best, and maybe the only, remaining framework for survival.

Your parents and professors have passed on to you the ideals and the intellectual habits that you need to shape your own world. Cherish them. They will serve you well whatever you do. Above all, do not be taken in by the arrogant myths of manhood or the trendy rhetoric of false feminism. For fame and wealth and power are no better or worse in themselves than their opposites—obscurity, poverty, and meekness. And, in the end, it matters little what you have or how prominent you become; it does matter what you are and that you follow your profession, whatever it be, with joy, intelligence, and enthusiasm.

Finally, never lose the enthusiasm of youth. Life grants us all innumerable opportunities to make our world a better place. One of the saddest things for those of us who pin our hopes for the future on youth, is to see young people stricken with premature rigidity, a form of psychological arteriosclerosis that restricts their vision and limits their potential. Yet, with a generous heart and an open mind—and it takes constant vigilance to keep that generosity and openness—you will find great delight in life.

Dreams and Travel
Journal of the Irish Colleges of Physicians and Surgeons,
1989

When a middle aged Jewish farmer in rural Wales experienced spiritual visions – the Paraclete twice appearing with instructions to "Become A Doctor" – it was fortunate that Harry O'Flanagan was Dean and Registrar of The Royal College of Surgeons in Ireland. It is difficult to imagine a more bizarre basis for applying to medical school, and the admissions interview must have been memorable. Flexibility, instinctive insights, and a bit of intellectual daring were characteristics of the O'Flanagan era at the College, and Asia, as well as Ireland, were the beneficiaries of this decision.

Jack Preger, the farmer with the visions, graduated from the College of Surgeons in 1971. After interning at St. Laurence's Hospital in Dublin, he pursued his dreams and established a practice among the poor, living in the sewer pipes of Bangladesh and later, under the bridges of Calcutta. His medical career is devoid of the graduate degrees, prestigious appointments, research articles, or material goods so often used as the crude criteria of success in our ancient and noble profession. In fact, Jack Preger seemed to have a penchant for conflict, and his highest honors can be measured in the inordinate amount of time be spent in Indian prisons fighting for the privilege to serve his forgotten slum dwellers. His story is the basis for these reflections on the international aspects of Irish medicine.

This small island nation has long enjoyed its rich reputation for travel. Celtic saints and scholars wandered far from the beaten path, teaching, proselytizing, and illuminating the darkness of the Middle Ages. The Wild Geese became Irish soldiers of fortune and explorers in the service of colonial powers; then, in a prescient change of loyalties, some shared in the early struggles for national independence throughout the tropics. Irish physicians and surgeons were partners in those journeys of discovery: the statue of Thomas H. Parke, M.D., the companion of Stanley and Emin Pasha through the wilds of Africa, stands guard before the National Library in Dublin, and spears collected on his travels are in my New York office. In modern times, missionary, government, voluntary agencies, and private business concerns, maintain an Irish medical influence in virtually every country of the Third World, offering a new generation opportunities for short-term service in established clinics and hospitals.

I believe that travel is an indispensable ingredient in the making of a good physician. Especially when young, at the student or registrar level, before one's approach to medicine becomes routine, and one set of facts is accepted as the only truth, it is important to go abroad. There the teachings of your revered – or feared – professors are not only challenged but ignored. It is humbling to work where one is a minority and learn that the easy assumptions of our society may be alien, and even offensive, to others. Contrast stimulates the mind, and comparisons enrich the resources each physician must eventually use to mold his or her future. One quickly learns – or, at least, one should – a critical lesson of life; that all roads run both ways, and great value can be gained as well as given in caring for the poor. The arrogant assumptions of modern medicine fade in the harsh realities of tropical life, and the young, Western trained physician almost inevitably returns as a more sensitive, mature, and patient person.

The cultural cross-fertilization that accompanies travel may well be the best bridge to peace and understanding in a troubled world. The visions of Jack Preger should be part of the curriculum of every Irish physician and student in the interdependent world of today.

A Necessary Balance
America, 1993

In 1729, the Dean of St. Patrick's Cathedral in Dublin, Jonathan Swift, in *A Modest Proposal for Preventing the Children of Poor People from Being a Burden to Their Parents,* suggested that the poverty stricken, famine threatened, and economically exploited Irish peasantry, who nonetheless produced such beautiful infants, could resolve the troubling specter of recurrent starvation by eating their own babies. In doing so, he argued, they might simultaneously address the complex, but related, social issues of overpopulation and malnutrition.

Maybe Swift's technique of proposing outlandish and obscene solutions in order to accentuate reality and subtly emphasize the need for more humane approaches is at play today as one follows the orchestrated suggestions that we should solve the current world's problems by creating yet another military force, this one under the aegis of the United Nations, an organization founded fifty years ago so that humanity could beat its swords into ploughshares.

Recently, Brian Urquhart, a former UN undersecretary general, embraced the concept of a standing UN army without even alluding to less violent means of resolving conflicts. Mr. Urquhart suggested that "a stillborn idea from the past may suggest an answer to our present world's crises"; maybe the earlier miscarriage was fortuitous. He declared that the United Nations is "now increasingly perceived and called upon as an international policeman and world emergency service," but he then failed to even mention or offer any suggestions for an expanded humanitarian component to balance the proposed new military undertaking. Is Brian Urquhart, the ultimate UN representative, a new Jonathan Swift? Maybe he is tweaking our moral senses with modern satire. If not, he seems to have abandoned hope that the world's peoples can reach a level of harmonious coexistence except when justice is dispensed at the end of a gun barrel.

There are many other examples in the present global minefield to document how readily world leaders convince themselves that more and more armed force will somehow break the cycle of ongoing revolution and violence. It is amazing how few voices of dissent are raised against such proposals. There is no doubt that military power—or at least the implicit threat of its use—may be an indispensable component in peacemaking operations, but it should always be recognized as the most costly and most transient approach to resolving the bitter ethnic, religious, racial, and economic differences at the core of so many current conflicts.

In Somalia the "solution" finally employed—after years of arming a brutal dictator and then neglecting all the signs of consequent oppression and anarchy—was an overwhelming exhibition of American military might. At a cost of $4 billion, the United States demonstrated that 35,000 armed American troops could temporarily prevent local warlords from killing innocent victims as well as each other. Six months after our orchestrated arrival in Mogadishu, and after months of television and media copy showing the satisfying images of famine being conquered – at least along the main thoroughfares – and of American troops returning safely home, we are once again indulging in dramatic displays of military power in Somalia, this time to "teach the local warlord a lesson." Whatever the domestic political objectives of this particular action may be, we are deceiving ourselves that such a simplistic approach is any substitute for the comprehensive rehabilitation needed in an utterly torn society.

Because we entered Somalia with a military mindset, it must have seemed acceptable to negotiate directly with local warlords, despite the obvious fact that their selfish and deadly battles had been responsible for the deaths of over 100,000 innocent Somalis. By our recognition we initially legitimized the position of General Aideed, while our latest invasion, and bungled attempt to arrest him, has unwittingly established Aideed as a new national hero in the tradition of Mohamed Abdille Hassan, the "Mad Mullah" who defended Somalia's integrity and sovereignty against the English in the early part of this century. In the eyes of many Somalis, accustomed to the rhetoric and actions of colonial masters, we have moved, in six short months, from a relief force to an army of occupation.

There are profound dangers in quick fix military solutions to complex problems. For example, is providing more arms to the Muslims in Bosnia really the most coherent solution that a great nation like the United States can offer to end a brutal civil war? Do we really want Libyan and Iranian arms to flow into Bosnia, further fueling the conflagration, so that we can sleep easily, knowing we have equaled the balance of weapons, thereby assuring that the killing, rape, and mutilation will inevitably escalate? Maybe President Clinton is simply utilizing the techniques of Dean Swift, and no one has yet detected the cruel joke.

Should a UN army intervene where there are violations of human rights or serious hazards to the health of an oppressed minority? It is generally conceded, for example, that the levels of starvation are currently higher in war-torn southern Sudan than those recorded in the worst times in Somalia. But there is a recognized and functioning government in the Sudan, and an armed UN intervention would almost certainly be rejected by, at the very least, all Third World nations that are keenly aware of how hard they had to fight recently to overthrow foreign colonialism and secure their own basic independence and sovereignty. Somalia, with its society and government in utter collapse, posed few legal complications when we finally acted, and it does not offer a precedent for future UN military actions.

The present crises in Yugoslavia, Somalia, and many other areas are not isolated events but are part of a vast panorama of change signaling the turbulent passage of history from one age to another. Most of the old premises of the international system are under siege. Fundamental principles such as national sovereignty, ideas that have stood for hundreds of years, are being challenged by a wide range of developments, from the communications revolution to popular mass movements. We cannot, for example, escape the devastating impact of epidemics, such as AIDS, that sweep across continents, attacking the rich as well as the poor. Today, television instantly imprints scenes of distant tragedies and gross human rights violations upon the world's consciousness and conscience, and we can no longer conveniently blot out such knowledge or deny an inevitable, even unwanted, involvement.

As Somalia has unequivocally demonstrated, disaster relief and humanitarian assistance have moved from the periphery to the center ring in foreign affairs. They can never again be considered merely minor matters to be relegated to well-meaning do-gooders, a balm to soothe the emotional outcry of a fickle citizenry.

Considerable attention has recently been given to the UN Secretary General's proposal to create a standing army based on designated troops that would be available from donor states on 24 hour notice. Brian Urquhart views this suggestion as only an interim measure, proposing instead a permanent UN army at the disposal of the Security Council. Under either system, the United Nations could, it is suggested, promptly respond to threats against, or breaches of, international peace and security, and the very existence of such an army might possibly have a sobering effect on would be aggressors.

One must question, however, whether the United Nations currently has the institutional capacity to administer a multilateral, culturally varied army. To function effectively, such a force would require, in the stress of battle, a level of coordination, integration, technical skill and command structure that has hardly characterized the UN efforts in simpler civilian undertakings. The very cost of training and maintaining thousand man voluntary contingents to be on call for UN use would automatically give the wealthy states a disproportionate say in determining how, when, and even which conflicts the United Nations will attempt to resolve. Furthermore, such an approach would be likely to exacerbate the bitter divisions between rich and poor nations that already are a prime cause of international tensions.

A more comprehensive, humane approach, one closer to the original idea of the United Nations, is imperative. The United Nations is the only global organization capable of promoting peace by non-violent means. In developing an improved military option, the United Nations should be careful not to sacrifice its meticulously constructed emphasis on basic human equality and fraternity. A military approach rarely, if ever, allows cooperation with the indigenous people in occupied lands, and military measures alone, unaccompanied by an effective humanitarian component, will only perpetuate a fundamentally flawed, and failed, method of resolving conflicts.

Even when political and diplomatic initiatives prove inadequate and armed intervention is considered necessary, such action should never be a strictly military operation. The plight of civilians caught up in war and disaster situations invariably requires immediate humanitarian assistance; in fact, this is the primary rationale usually offered to justify military involvement. The international community now has a rare opportunity to ensure a better balance between its military and humanitarian obligations. Not to insist on this linkage would be catastrophic for future generations. Power will inevitably flow where the money is, and the present UN budgetary rules will guarantee that the military option will prevail. In fact, the peacekeeping costs for 1992–93 are already 50 percent more than the regular budget of the entire rest of the UN organization.

Chapter 7 of the UN Charter provides for mandatory assessments to support military operations, but it only encourages Member States to cooperate voluntarily in, and offer aid for, humanitarian efforts. Consequently, in many disaster situations, UN assistance is late and insufficient. The General Assembly has sought to correct this inequity by establishing the office of Undersecretary General for Humanitarian Affairs. With much initial fanfare, $50 million was voluntarily subscribed by donor countries as an operational fund for the new department's worldwide activities. To put that sum in perspective, it should be noted that the annual budget for the UN activities in the former Yugoslavia is over $3 billion, and that the budget for the local New York State Health and Human Services Department is over $30 billion. Furthermore, despite the lofty title, the new Undersecretary General of Humanitarian Affairs has not been given a clear mandate. Too often such separate UN empires as the World Health Organization, the United Nations Children's Emergency Fund, the United Nations Office of the High Commissioner for Refugees, and the United Nations Development Program end up as competing forces in a field where coordination and leadership are essential.

While war, famine, disease, epidemics and other life threatening calamities increasingly call for international intervention, the UN agencies responsible for relief operations are obliged to engage in a constant round of begging in order to obtain food, medicine, and other critically needed supplies. That approach is becoming more and more difficult. Donor exhaustion and donor distraction are well known reactions to repetitive humanitarian appeals. It will undoubtedly be exacerbated if donor countries feel their obligations have already been satisfied by military contributions to UN peacekeeping operations.

The humanitarian operations of the United Nations should be put on the same financial footing as the peacekeeping operations, and these costs should be recognized as legitimate expenses within the meaning of Article 7 of the Charter. Such a decision would not preclude additional charitable contributions. The United Nations' role as the only viable coordinator in most disasters would be enormously strengthened, and the world community would at last be able to channel its caring and compassion into an efficient system, one that would replace the competing and often politically motivated approaches that now tarnish so many relief efforts.

The Secretary General could organize the humanitarian contingents along the same lines proposed for the UN standing army. Member States could be asked to train, equip, and maintain rapid response disaster relief teams. Sweden, Norway, and Switzerland have already established such teams, and it should not be difficult to identify doctors, nurses, engineers, and other necessary personnel in most of the donor countries that are now being asked to supply only military troops.

In the early stages of disasters, the military is singularly equipped to play a critical role. No other group has the needed discipline and coordination, much less the essential equipment such as helicopters and field hospitals. An early military response illustrates how the United Nations can adapt to serve humanitarian needs, with an army being used as the "iron fist in a velvet glove" approach. Relief programs, however, are the major tool for overcoming military and diplomatic impasses and for promoting attempts at reconciliation in areas where, and at times when, mutual suspicion and even hatred prevail.

The failure to appreciate both the primacy and the potential of humanitarian efforts is a recurring tragedy that prolongs civilian suffering and hinders the rehabilitation process. Changing a humanitarian effort into a security action may offer a temporary respite from the pain of frustration, but if reflects an approach that, while gratifying the short term needs of the healer, fails to resolve the problems of the patient. The vast scope of military operations inevitably alters the critical relationship between donor and recipient, drains the finite resources available, and imposes a transient mirage of well being that simply cannot be sustained.

By cooperating on recognized health problems, it is sometimes possible for deadly enemies to share in alleviating the wounds of war. By identifying common grounds, such efforts can reduce misunderstandings and help begin that difficult, but essential journey, one that allows enemies to become reluctant citizens and, eventually, cooperative neighbors. Military and humanitarian components must be seen as equal partners in a coherent program worthy of the ideals of the United Nations. The news from around the world makes this more evident each day.

A Dublin Department
2006

In 1969 an independent Department of Tropical Medicine was established at the Royal College of Surgeons in Ireland (RCSI). I was appointed as Professor and Chairman. My own involvement with the College began almost a decade earlier. In 1960, one of my first formal medical lectures was delivered on *Hepatitis in Pregnancy* at RCSI's Jervis Street Hospital. I was working at the time as a Research Fellow for Professor Shelia Sherlock at the Royal Free Hospital in London. Professor Sherlock arranged an invitation for me to visit Ireland, at least in part so that I could have a much desired reunion with my fiancée.

One of the problems with this maiden lecture at the RCSI was its timing: four o'clock on December 24th. Halfway through my undoubtedly overly serious talk, replete with slides of destroyed organs and dying women, a somewhat inebriated observer said, "For God's sake, Mister, will you sit down, it's Christmas Eve." Even if the audience may have long forgotten the hepatologic details presented, I certainly remember that introduction to the College. I also learned a very important lesson on appropriate timing in academia.

A number of years later, in 1964, as a young physician serving as Head of the Department of Epidemiology and Director of Clinical Tropical Medicine for the U.S. Navy at a Research Institute in Egypt, I was invited by the legendary Registrar of the RCSI, Dr. Harry O'Flanagan, to revisit the College. After an obvious trial of a lecture on leishmaniasis, he asked that I consider the position of Professor of Tropical Medicine and submit a formal curriculum for faculty consideration. Lecturers were soon identified, and a detailed budget was even provided. There were, however, several obstacles and it took five years to reach resolution, evidence of the leisurely pace of Irish negotiations in the 1960s, and of my own determination to create a Department that would survive.

If a course in tropical medicine was merely an adjunct in a Department of Microbiology, Pathology, Public Health or Medicine, it would, I believed, be an easy sacrificial lamb in the cauldron that characterizes curriculum negotiations. I argued that tropical medicine was a unique discipline, not merely parasitology or epidemiology or exotic infectious diseases. I insisted that there be a separate Department, that tropical medicine not be an elective course, but a requirement for all training to become physicians in an international world, and that the final assessment be a "stopping exam" so that students could not graduate until they passed our test.

When the College, in 1969, finally accepted my suggestions, I assumed the Chairmanship of a new fledging Department. A proper foundation was now in place and the College leadership was most supportive. Much was to be accomplished over the next thirty-six years from these humble beginnings. The Department's birth coincided with Ireland's growing involvement in international aid and it became a critical advisory resource. Collaborative links with religious organizations were also fostered.

The mandatory course in tropical medicine at the RCSI has been, since its inception, the most extensive program offered in any medical school in Europe or the United States of America. The RCSI also operates medical schools in Malaysia, Bahrain and Dubai. Over the first decade the Department developed an array of postgraduate Diploma courses, a Travel Health Center, a semi-annual journal, an overseas elective scheme for medical students, collaborative courses with other European colleges, and a museum of tropical medicine, a visual arts center with anatomical specimens and slides from around the world.

Personal Reflections

I conclude this review of my thirty-six year tenure as Professor and Chairman with both fond memories and great confidence. To create a new Department within a medical school such as the RCSI, one rich in history and tradition, is indeed a privilege. My initial lecture was attended by Professor Alan Thompson, a remarkable Quaker physician who had worked with Samuel Beckett in the ruins of Saint-Lô after World War II. Great figures in College history, such as Presidents A.B. Cleary and Terence Millin, were in attendance at my opening lecture, and their service to Irish medicine dated back to the 1920s.

My own tenure is not even the longest in College history; Arthur Jacob was Head of Anatomy for forty years. Nevertheless, as I reflect back over more than three and a half decades within the College, having taught over 4000 undergraduates, and hundreds of postdoctoral candidates, I am quite satisfied that my successor inherits a solid base from which the RCSI will continue to fulfill its global destiny.

Many years ago I wrote a letter to a lecturer in the Department, struggling to define his own path forward in Irish medicine. I found a copy of that letter while clearing out my office files, and portions of it aptly capture my own deep feeling about the essential ethos of our College:

Most of us who make our living in the private practice of medicine do not—and cannot—accurately calculate the benefit or the value of our unpaid service to the Hippocratic tradition of teaching new generations our ancient arts. The very essence of the RCSI is teaching and establishing qualifications—that is why it was founded hundreds of years ago, why so many men and women have, over the centuries, proudly devoted themselves to its development, usually without any (or a miniscule) salary.

Establishing competing courses in our discipline, when every effort has been made to concentrate such activities in order to foster excellence at RCSI, does strike at the very core of what allows a College to thrive generation after generation. Understanding this unwritten academic ethos is neither a legal nor moral obligation but it is, it seems to me, as binding and essential as trust in a good marriage. Without the confidence and respect of colleagues within the academic community, free standing teaching courses are unlikely to long survive; their inability to grant degrees, or be accepted as international qualifications, are fundamental flaws. More importantly, the isolation which such courses can elicit may deceive, and even harm, the very students one is supposedly serving.

I offer these reflections with the same understanding, respect and fatherly affection, that I recall as the tone and theme of a long conversation we once had on a walk along Harcourt Street. Eventually, one of the two paths that lie before you must be chosen—either one accepts the role of the College, and the dreams of this Professor, to centralize tropical medicine and international health within our Department, or one embarks on an entrepreneurial venture divorced from our own academic base.

If you follow the former path I believe all those qualities cited at the beginning of this letter will bring you the respect and reputation you deserve. If you view your service solely on a sessional basis, without understanding and accepting my goals, and the traditions of academia, you may financially succeed in the short run, but I humbly suggest you will unnecessarily jeopardize your own potential.

As I retire from the Department of International Health and Tropical Medicine, the College has created a new Chair in International Humanitarian Affairs. I have accepted that Professorship, hoping to extend the helpful and healing outreach of our ancient College to the new humanitarian crises that scar our world.

Is That All There Is?
2006

After completing medical school most young doctors become "residents" for three to four years in a hospital where they learn specialist skills; some then go on for another two to three years training as "fellows."

I am pleased and honored to be asked to share in this graduation ceremony, for those who have, finally, completed their postdoctoral program. Maybe the much awaited promotions and appointments, the barely suppressed dreams of professional success, are what you now want, and probably richly deserve. After the many years of long days and nights of hospital service, and the necessary isolated life that characterize medical training, you have every right to look forward to, among other things, the material rewards that can soon be yours, allowing you to pay off debts and establish independent lives. You move on, up, acquire new titles, new responsibilities, new positions of power, directing training programs for the next lot of residents and fellows, maintaining a noble tradition that dates back thousands of years.

But is that all there is? Does that fulfill your deepest desires? Because you wear a stethoscope do you cut off other paths, other roles as a citizen? Does being a physician preclude being an artist, or a poet, a sculptor or a philosopher, a gardener or an explorer? Is being a physician, even a very good physician, an adequate foundation to face the challenges, and opportunities, that are both inevitable and unpredictable?

One of the lessons I learned very early, in the chaos that characterizes life in refugee camps, is that the medical contribution is but a small part of the puzzle. Many decades ago I came to appreciate that our vaunted professional medical role was usually the easy part. To be a healer, when no one else could offer help, was usually quite simple, very satisfying, but, one quickly learned, if one were honest, that it had a very transient impact. Establishing a good clinic, or even a fully functioning public health system, is poor satisfaction to the vulnerable mothers and children who are exposed to constant physical threats.

In the late 1950s a young and idealistic American physician was dispensing modern medicine in the hills of Laos and Cambodia. Tom Dooley – I knew him as he died at New York Hospital while I was a student – was almost sanctified by the media because, in that pre-Vietnam War era, he offered an image of help in South East Asia. But his efforts, so impressive to innocent journalists who didn't understand the basics of public health, had almost no impact, and, when he left, nothing lasting remained.

Many times, as I directed very large refugee camps in Somalia, or after the 1972 earthquake in Nicaragua, when I tried to bring order to a medical system in a city where 25,000 people had died in a midnight cataclysm, or in the almost bizarre confusion of the southern Sudan where I once served, for many lonely months, as the only physician in an area the size of New England, I discovered that I needed tent makers and truck drivers, sanitary engineers, canal and well diggers, security forces, and laborers to dispose of the dead, more than additional doctors or nurses. At the very least, I surely, and quickly, came to know that I needed other practical skills far more than the diagnostic and therapeutic input that most physicians see as their expected contribution.

I am not demeaning the role of medicine. In fact, I would like to suggest that, far too often, we underestimate our potential. But in those complex humanitarian crises that have become the common, tragic interface between the developed and developing worlds, we must broaden the definition of our discipline or, as physicians, we will inevitably fail to fulfill our most basic obligations.

You have trained in medicine to think in an almost unique way, to try to solve problems quickly, to make life and death decisions in the urgent settings of an ER or an ICU. You have been taught to learn from failures, to study autopsy material so that you not repeat the errors – often iatrogenic – that lead to unnecessary death. In Morbidity and Mortality Meetings you have become accustomed to present facts – even unpleasant facts – openly and honestly so that future patients may survive.

In daily bedside rounds, and weekly conferences, seminars and symposia you have come to know the importance of sharing knowledge, of learning how to work cooperatively so that you can chart a coherent regimen from multiple, diverse, often conflicting and even competing, data, and how to deal with dated ideas, and the strong, sometimes rigid, personalities of senior colleagues. Have you ever thought how rare this approach is in the world? Do people in business or diplomacy, in military or religious life – does any other discipline – try to solve universal problems with the intellectual and emotional tools you have been trained to now take for granted?

I can assure you our approach, our inherited medical ethos and logic, is very unusual indeed, especially when the egos of national leaders are involved. Tropical medicine brought me at an early age to areas where great epidemics decimated whole populations. Endless wars not only killed innocent civilians, but caused the death of whole societies. Conflicts prevented planting and harvesting of crops, and destroyed the essential breeding cycles for animals, leading to mass, man-made famines. Health services collapsed, and insect control programs were abandoned, causing a resurgence of diseases we once dreamed of eradicating. In the areas of sub-Saharan Africa that I came to know so well, malaria, tuberculosis, and other utterly preventable diseases still snuff out young lives on a scale that is almost incomprehensible.

Yet this was where I found myself – first in Calcutta in 1959, then for five wondrous years in Egypt, Somalia and the southern Sudan, and then, over the last forty years as a part of Lenox Hill Hospital's global mission, making frequent research and relief journeys to war or conflict zones on every continent. I didn't expect to be in these situations, and there certainly were no lectures in my medical school or hospital training that prepared me for such challenges. But I would like to again suggest that we – you and I privileged to work as physicians – may be better armed than most any other profession to be flexible, to know when and how to adapt, to sometimes even be able to unravel the causes of conflicts, and discover those elusive paths to healing the wounds and scars of traumatized populations.

I have worked with humanitarian and diplomatic leaders around the world, and today there is a growing consensus that the failed approaches of the past will certainly fail again. Power politics and military actions may provide transient satisfaction; but, to have any lasting effect, such efforts must be coordinated with health and human rights and educational improvements. Health workers are, therefore, major partners if justice and peace, stability and development are to be realized. Physicians simply must assume new responsibilities in a world where another failure could prove to be the final act of civilization.

In my own experience, compassion and charity did not always prevail, but identifying, and establishing, common ground in the chaos of conflicts offered a reason, and a time, and a place, where hatreds could be temporarily put aside. When all else had failed we did create transient zones of tranquility. International pressure and aid can usually be generated to support such efforts. It is during such lulls that one can initiate that difficult process which may well begin in argument, but can evolve into civilized dialogue and, eventually, allow those shared efforts that are indispensable in the reconstruction of a torn society. Such a path has great risks, but establishing a firm foundation for diplomacy out of the human tragedies and political failures of the past is an approach we must pursue. There are very few options left.

Based on these experiences I proposed, at a United Nations conference in the early 1990s, that we in medicine and public health had something fundamental to offer to the softer discipline of diplomacy, a field that prefers rhetoric to reality, and certainly avoids critical self-examination. I then wrote a book, modestly entitled *Preventive Diplomacy: Stopping Wars Before They Start,* whose thesis has been adopted by the Swedish government as a formal part of their foreign policy. Sweden now analyzes every international decision to see whether prevention, rather than merely reaction, might work. They have used whole pages from my Introduction to fashion their law, no mean satisfaction for a physician who dared to step out of our self-imposed professional constraints, seeing negotiations on diplomatic and political issues as essential a part of my role in a refugee program as providing food or shelter or drugs.

I would like to conclude with several related observations. As physicians you have an enormous, untapped reservoir of legitimacy and credibility. Never abandon your medical base. There is no substitute for clinical practice. It offers a unique position from which you can appreciate the realities and wonder of life, and, if handled with decency and dignity, you can win the respect of people of all races and creeds and political beliefs. The constant challenges, the humbling failures, the unreasonable demands, the slings and arrows of clinical life, participating in the joys and sorrows of birth and pain, healing and death, are your daily privileges.

I hope that you too can find this eternal radiance in life, and look around at a world in desperate need of your help, and then have the courage to step out of the box.

Do not be frightened by the unknown, or shy away from challenges that were not part of your training, for you will quickly realize that others on the scene have no greater capacity, and, in fact, have usually had a much more narrow educational base. Do not place false restrictions on, or in any way limit, your options. If you can translate the ethos of our profession to a world starved for order and competency, social justice and the rights of the frail and oppressed—and that is what the Hippocratic oath encourages you to do—then, when opportunity presents, and it will in the most unexpected and exciting ways, do not let it escape out of some foolish concern for the secure career path that today seems to offer the satisfactions and rewards you rightly consider your due for a job well done.

Congratulations on completing this stage in your training, and God speed on the incredibly rich journey ahead, one that awaits your full participation.

Part Three: Continuity

I was one of eight children raised in a loving but slightly dysfunctional home dominated by my Jesuit trained father, a physician who recited Latin and Greek poetry as bedtime lullabies. He insisted, if we wanted his attention on any serious matter, that we "put it on paper" declaring that "if it's important enough to you then write it down." I never forgot that lesson.

I have written or edited thirty-three books and over two hundred medical and other articles on a wide range of topics, all important to me. My first book on clinical tropical medicine was written over fifty years ago and is still in use, in its eighth edition. This, and other technical texts, reflect an essential and integral part of my work, but excerpts from them do not fit in this broader, more philosophic book. The pieces chosen for this section cover a wide range of subjects but are linked, in an evolutionary way, by a number of constant and recurring themes. I present here parts of Introductions and a Conclusion from a series of linked volumes. I have placed the pieces in chronological order. In retrospect I see how much innocence there was in some of these attempts to change the world.

For example, rereading The AIDS Epidemic *thirty three years after it was written brings back those early days when we suspected, on the basis of some five hundred plus cases in New York City, that a new, puzzling disease might grow in significance. This was the first book published on AIDS, and it was translated into many languages. We did not then know the cause of AIDS, and effective therapy was more a wish than a reality. Nonetheless, the book did suggest a way forward and the lessons of an early epidemic remain valid.*

Many varied topics were covered in these books, joined, I would suggest, by the mixture of passion and compassion that has characterized my actions. For example, the forceful response to draconian budget cuts covered in Imminent Peril: Public Health in a Declining Economy *resulted in the restoration of over $50 million to a decimated health budget.*

A good summary of my own half-century obsession with the struggles of the poor and oppressed are offered in Traditions, Values and Humanitarian Action. *The piece from* Technology for Humanitarian Action *is another effort in the continuous struggle to find better ways to help people survive, and live in dignity, good health, and freedom.*

Over the past three decades my focus has been on establishing academic standards for training personnel to deal effectively with the complex challenges of humanitarian crises. I have written or edited thirteen volumes published by Fordham University Press; seven have been translated into French. Fordham's Institute of International Humanitarian Affairs has now over 2,000 graduates from 133 nations.

I conclude this section with excerpts from three more recent texts to demonstrate the continuity of thought that links my present work with earlier efforts.

Sometimes I feel guilty realizing how much joy and pleasure I found in what, for many, would seem to be the wastelands of the earth. After a hard few months' work among a large refugee population, my wife joined me for a tour of ten remote camps. One of the symbols for fertility in Somalia is an ostrich egg; here my wife, already the mother of five sons, had just received her fourth egg of the day.

Her warm, infectious smile made it all seem so natural and easy to both her husband and the local general.

Health on the Horn of Africa
1969

The eastern Horn of Africa is the land of the Somalis. It is a harsh, arid land whose culture reflects an existence geared to an eternal struggle for survival. All aspects of life revolve today, as they have for centuries, around the semiannual monsoon seasons and the success or failure of the rains.

Water is the crux of the economy, the synonym for beauty, the common thread of all cultural expression, and the greatest single factor influencing health on the Horn. In the dry savannah and semidesert plains that cover almost 80 percent of Somalia, men and their herds migrate endlessly from pasturage to pasturage. Only the hardiest nomads and animals survive. Fertile strips of arable land border the two rivers coursing through southern Somalia. The Juba and Uebi Scebeli both originate in the Ethiopian highlands and flow southeastward to the Indian Ocean. It is the interriverine agricultural area that still holds the major hope for a viable economic future.

Despite its strategic coastline, stretching for 2,600 miles along the Gulf of Aden and down the Indian Ocean, few foreigners sought to influence this unyielding corner of Africa, and even fewer succeeded in doing so. Persians, Turks, Arabs, Portuguese, and armies of the Sultan of Zanzibar held coastal enclaves in Somalia at various times from the fifteenth to the nineteenth centuries, but none were able to penetrate and conquer the interior. Just as their extensive desert borders effectively isolated the Somalis from surrounding African tribes, so also did their fierce pride prevent assimilation of other migrants who landed on their shores. None of the many coastal settlers significantly influenced the mores of the Somalis except for the profound impact of the Arab introduction of Islam. An intensely poetic, physically beautiful people, the Somalis long ago learned to share in order to survive. The very word *so maal* means "welcome, and milk my beast"—a generous greeting that I have known at remote wells and shall not forget.

As the twentieth century began, therefore, the eastern Horn was unique in Africa. It was occupied by a nation of people with one language, one religion, and one cultural heritage, living mainly a nomadic life that was basically similar throughout the Horn.

It was their land when Queen Hatshepsut sent expeditions there 3,500 years ago to obtain frankincense trees. It was their land when the white man came and drew artificial boundaries on paper maps that meant nothing to the Somali nomad. Colonial politicians could carve up a continent, coastline conquerors could come and go, but the nomad in the interior knew none of this, for his life was spent in a lonely, endless search for water.

Sir Richard Burton, the first Englishman to travel deeply in the Horn, described the Somalis as "a fierce race of Republicans, the Irish of Africa." In addition to their obvious love of the land the Somalis had other typical Celtic qualities, those of unquestioned, if not occasionally injudicious, bravery, articulateness, and humor, coupled with a great respect for poetry, democracy, age, and religion. Above all, they had a fanatic pride in Somalia and the Somalis. Burton noted "they are full of curiosity and travel the world accepting almost any job without feeling a sense of inferiority, perhaps because they believe that they are superior to everyone else." Their contact with neighbors was limited largely to warfare, and they survived, untarnished by the turbulent development of emerging Africa or the progress of the Western and Eastern worlds. Their independence had been secured by isolation.

As the pace of colonization in Africa quickened toward the end of the nineteenth century, the Somalis felt, for the first time the grip of the European conqueror. Although the grasp tightened, under one aegis or the other over the next half century, it still had a surprisingly small impact on the social or cultural life of the Somalis.

During the first forty years of the 20th century, the Italians ruled the southern part of Somalia with major garrisons along the Indian Ocean from Chisamiyu to Cape Guardafui, and inland along the Uebi Scebelli and Juba rivers. But the garrisons were there to protect Italian interests, and little was done to alter the indigenous beliefs or customs of the Somalis in fields such as education or medicine. The same was true of the English area along the Gulf of Aden and the highlands of the north, as well as in the French settled port of Djibouti. Welfare programs were not a feature of colonial governments at this time. The vagaries of international politics since the mid 1930s made this early neglect in native welfare programs almost appear positive.

Mussolini launched his transient dream for an Italian East African empire from Somalia. The pressures of initial conquest and later retreat and surrender precluded the development of much in the way of "native services." When the English army assumed control of all Somalia in 1941, they did so only as a holding operation, and the continuity of planning and administration necessary for social programs was wanting. Even during the UN Trusteeship of ex-Italian Somalia from 1950–60, higher priorities were—sometimes for justifiable reasons—given to the development of programs of economy and security than those of health. In the British protectorate to the north, developments in this sphere were equally rare.

Independence in 1960 brought no magical solutions to the problems of Somalia. In fact, in many ways, all were accentuated by inexperience, incompetence, a materialism newly discovered by its leaders, and widespread corruption. A mass exodus of expatriate professional personnel put tremendous strain on the very basic social programs of the new nation. This was particularly evident in the field of health; for example, every foreign medical doctor left northern Somaliland within a week of independence.

I know the Somalis well. Ours is a relationship forged in hardship. During many medical trips to every part of the Horn I have known their joy, hopes, and failures. I have cared for them during epidemics and in periods of flood and drought. I have traveled the bush for weeks on end with the nomads, sharing their meals while tracking their diseases. I have come away with an enormous respect for their strength and loyalty, their kindness to the stranger, their silent wisdom, and their knowledge of nature and the stars and the hot winds.

They can offer—as desert folk are wont to do—generous and gentle hospitality, while showing the qualities of toughness, shrewdness, and fatalism that make survival possible in an environment best described by their great national poet and leader, Mohamed Abdile Hassan:

Bush, thick and impenetrable, scorched
hagar trees, the hot air rising from them,
Hot wind and heat, which will lick
you like a flame,

A mantle of air and a shade giving
tree to shelter you
The swelling of feet pricked by thorns,
a thorny thicket, plants prickly and spiny.

The life of a camel herder may be hard, but the verities cited by Mohamed Abdile Hassan are still valid. There are truths that do not change with time, and realities that will not bend with the winds of political expediency.

Who welcomes you like a kinsman
in your day of need
And who at the height of the
drought
does not bar his gate against
you
Is not he who never fails you in
your weakness one of your
brethren?

The Somalis will know—and will remember—those who reached out in their day of need and those who barred the gate against their dreams and watched them fail. They will know their brethren.

*One of the constant themes in my life has
been the need to build on the trust and
credibility medicine allows and to use
that foundation to present an image of the
United States that is poorly understood in
most developing nations. Diplomats are
not defined merely by titles.*
*They include all who can help translate
and present out national character, goals,*

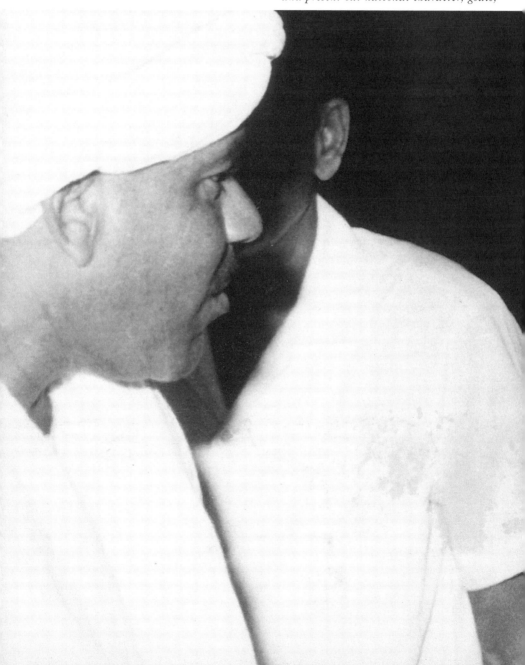

and frustrations to other people.
This communication should be a dialogue,
not merely an assertion of power based
on the false, and ultimately self-defeating,
premise that somehow only we know
what is right.
This photo captures an effort to convince
some African and Arab representatives
after I had spoken at a UN gathering.

My lovely wife was, on most occasions, the
more impressive and memorable partner in
our efforts.

The Untapped Resource
1971

Medicine is one of the last, and certainly the most promising, untapped resources in contemporary international diplomacy. That is the unqualified contention of *The Untapped Resource*, published at a critical time. The future of foreign assistance programs is being debated. Alternatives to unsuccessful approaches in international relations are being sought. Funds for international medical research are diminishing. A "new" diplomacy is emerging in an era of instant communications. It is to be hoped that we in the developed countries have the maturity, the wisdom, and, if necessary, the courage to jettison the standard, rigidly pursued, and often unsuccessful practices of past foreign policy in order to seek new methods of presenting what is fine and decent in our nation to a hostile world. If life is a series of alternatives, then medicine represents a good one for diplomacy.

In today's world of newly emerging nations and powerful ideological blocs, diplomacy is restricted by few traditions and assumes many unorthodox guises. As the nations of the Third World became independent, Eastern and Western superpowers wooed them with every conceivable form of aid. Many new governments have consistently accepted these "grants" with a gratitude marked by a lingering suspicion that the giver covertly seeks only his own good. Thus, the foreign airport builder or road maker may find his efforts cited as proof of the militaristic nature of his "colonialist government." The agriculture attaché can be accused of destroying traditional farming methods, the dam builder of flooding the land, and the teacher of indoctrinating or deluding the young.

Few areas of overseas aid are immune to the sensitivities and misinterpretations of recipient nations. Few forms of aid can be offered with the assurance that both donor and recipient will experience the dramatic impact of immediate benefit, as well as the long-term effect of hard won mutual respect. Few projects can be completed with the assurance that later political changes will not confuse or diminish the good that was done. Medicine is a unique exception, especially in the Third World where infectious diseases and epidemics remain the great scourges.

Medicine and diplomacy are neither strange nor recent partners. Ancient kings employed their physicians as ambassadors of good will. The trust, respect, and affection elicited by the professional medical man was not limited to his role in the relief of pain or the control of disease, but extended to those he represented – his nation and his people. In many modern nations at the time of independence the doctor and the clergyman were the only educated members of the community and played prominent roles in national and international affairs. The role of the doctor in politics and foreign affairs in modern Latin American and African nations is well known.

For many years, the average citizen has been content to relegate foreign affairs to the nebulous realms of the State Department. But that time is gone. No longer can foreign policy be the exclusive domain of striped pants ambassadors and their staffs. Today, the masses in every nation forcefully project their feelings, and statesmen must be responsive to these demands. American youth, for example, is taking a significant international role, through the Peace Corps and other exchange programs; only the most bemused official would not take advantage of this obviously sincere desire to serve their fellow man.

What is needed at every level of government is not only leadership and direction, but also motivation and understanding. Anyone working in, or even visiting, a foreign country becomes involved–willingly or unwillingly – in the political exchange of his native and host nations. Even those who remain at home have a critical role in foreign policy, since their taxes pay for overseas programs and they elect legislators whose views on foreign policy are a crucial part of any political platform. The "diplomacy of the masses" is here to stay.

We all have, whether we like it or not, heavy responsibilities to encourage and foster better international understanding. Otherwise, we must be willing to face the inevitable consequences of future war, cold or hot, further suffering, and the tragic sacrifice of so much human and material potential. I have had the privilege of intimate contact with numerous diplomatic efforts while being associated with, and later directing, American medical research teams working in tropical areas. From these experiences I became convinced that combining medicine and diplomacy represents a most natural vehicle for modern international communication. In Africa, for example, where the stability of governments is yet a rare phenomenon, my own medical work served to form a bond between several regimes. In one country, I had the pleasure of working under three different governments, caring for successive Prime Ministers, and there have been times when all three sought my assistance in transmitting highly confidential messages to leaders in the United States.

Physicians and medical workers have the unique opportunity of entering far more rapidly than any other profession into the closed and often suspicious inner political circles and power structures of developing lands. Needless to say, this privilege brings responsibility and requires great sensitivity and understanding on the part of the physician-diplomat. If a program of medical aid is to be a vehicle for a diplomatic effort, it must be entrusted to extremely wise physicians who are not only highly competent in their own profession but are also alert to the limitations of diplomatic relations. They must have the courage to bridge the transient, but often superficial, differences that so often separate nations.

Not all overseas medical ventures are helpful in furthering international understanding. There are many painful examples of wasted and misguided effort. During several years as a physician in Egypt, the major clinical research program sponsored by an American navy unit was on zinc metabolism in Egyptian dwarfs. Egyptian physicians and politicians alike asked if that program was purposely selected to offend, since it must have represented the most miniscule health program of that struggling land. How much better it would have been – for medicine, for Egypt, for America – to concern ourselves with the major endemic illnesses of Egypt. Such diseases are rare in our country and difficult to investigate here.

We could, and clearly should, have utilized our unique presence in the very center of a troubled area by identifying ourselves with, for example, the problem of infant diarrhea, which is responsible for over 50 percent of childhood mortality in Egypt. Adjacent to the American research station where I was the Director of Tropical Medicine was a local 1,500 bed fever hospital. Yet when I began work there, no cooperative studies had been undertaken for many years, and a rusted lock prevented admission.

With what arrogance did we decide on a study of zinc metabolism which, if it were to be done at all, could be more readily and more effectively accomplished in the sophisticated laboratories of our own country? Why should such a research program dominate the only American biochemistry and clinical facilities in an area crying for help against infectious diseases that kill and maim hundreds of thousands annually? In this case a health program not only failed to help international goodwill; it irritated an open wound of misunderstanding and distrust.

In other overseas health projects, the physician as well as the bureaucrat must bear the burden for past failures. Medical men have often been unwilling or incapable of demanding that the health aspects of developmental projects be considered at every phase of planning and execution. Health must be recognized as integral a part of any human development scheme as are engineering, economic, or agricultural components.

In Africa, several large dam and irrigation projects were completed before the nations became aware – by both human and animal disease and death – of the catastrophic problems produced when the natural ecology is altered and various vectors of disease are permitted to multiply and spread. This failure of physicians to articulately present their knowledge in words that are acceptable and understandable to legislators, politicians, and business leaders is no longer tolerable. The men of medicine can no longer abdicate their professional responsibilities nor fail their obligations as citizens of the world.

It is the physicians' code – and it is a good one – to insist that programs dealing with our profession grow from experience and be presented first to our peers. Only then, if proven relevant, should programs be made available for consideration and enactment by the lay public. This program – linking medicine and diplomacy – began while I was working in the Middle East, Africa, and Asia. This concept of combining medicine and diplomacy grew to a conviction that I first presented to a medical audience six years ago; it then blossomed into a symposium published by *The Bulletin of the New York Academy of Medicine*.

Having allowed the concept to develop from intuition to

conviction, having tested the theory in practice, having secured the interest and following of a highly competent group of medical leaders, it seems to me time to present this idea as forcefully as possible to the lay public and, in particular, to the legislators who determine and enact our foreign policy. America, and the entire developed world, has paid lip service to the health needs of the vast population the Third World. Lip service will no longer suffice.

Another myth plaguing international medicine is the easy solution of the unknowing, relegating all global health problems to the World Health Organization (WHO). One need only point out that the budget of the New York Health Department is more than ten times that of the WHO. The WHO itself makes no claim to handling major medical problems around the world. It attempts, primarily, to be an advisory and coordinating service, and this it does very well. However, that hardly meets our need for a new vehicle for international exchanges nor the developing world's need for medical assistance programs at every level.

The marriage of medicine and diplomacy is a realistic, feasible and economically sound goal, and I suggest will be inevitable in the decades ahead.

Irish Essays
1980

My father was a physician who, not incidentally, knew more poetry – and could recite it with more intense passion and feeling – than anyone I have ever met. Undoubtedly, I absorbed his view of the world, if not by osmosis then surely by forced participation, while traveling on medical house calls in the Irish immigrant neighborhoods of the Bronx.

Family and clan were all important then, for one turned inward (in that pre-television era) for support, love, entertainment, and solace. When one finally emerged from that beautiful shelter, it was with a broad interest in almost every human activity and with a belief that there were few, if any, natural boundaries. Medicine was not merely a technical science; it was a great art. Politics was patently too important an activity to leave to any "authority." The purpose of all our education was to widen and strengthen our interests, not to narrow our talents; specific training for any discipline would come soon enough, but it should never be mistaken for thought.

Much of this Irish interest lay latent in my genes and was quickened by romantic tales heard around the kitchen table in my youth. Later, an interest in the history of medicine led back to Ireland, and a fortuitous academic appointment drew me into close association with medical colleagues there. These experiences soon led from the lecture theater, through contacts with students and patients, to an awareness of the ills of Ireland. I came to know not only Ireland's beauty but her terrible torment. I also came to see both love and hatred there.

The evils of Ireland cry out to the international community for help; local remedies having utterly failed. Yet the physician must believe that the festering wounds of Ulster are not incurable. The body politic in Northern Ireland, the structure of government, has collapsed, and a semblance of order is maintained only by armed force. The symptoms of serious disease abound, and the diagnosis is not difficult. Yet, despite spasmodic efforts, those responsible have not provided any effective therapy. To stay uninvolved, to sit silently by, particularly when my background and present positions presented unique opportunities to serve, would have been a denial of instinct, of conscience and, in my judgment, of professional duty.

The bitter legacy of history will not suddenly disappear from Northern Ireland. Ancient differences will not die, and old hatreds will take a long time to fade. But tolerance, and the community of shared interests on which it is built, have been achieved in even more difficult situations. We already know the harm done by inaction and neglect in Northern Ireland. The present policy of permitting a glacial resolution to its problems is merely a sentence of violent death for future generations of Irish children. It displays a fatalistic despair that Britain and America have rejected in every other domestic and international problem they have faced. There are historic reasons why a continued American dimension in Northern Ireland is inevitable, and for strong moral and pragmatic reasons that dimension is fully consistent with current U.S. foreign policy. There are ample precedents to justify – and indeed encourage – a strong American political and economic contribution to this struggle for peace and justice.

America, more than any other nation, knows that civil unrest and riots are fed by economic and social oppression. Violence is a symptom of social disorder; treat the disease and violence subsides. Give people an effective voice in government and an opportunity to fashion a decent life for themselves, and they will not turn to those who seek to rule through intimidation. History, reason, and common sense support this belief and give the lie to hopeless resignation in the face of difficulties that, after all, are man made and must be solved by man. For if history holds one clear lesson for us, it is that when leaders refuse to use constitutional means to achieve justice, revolutionaries will use violent means. And conversely, if men of peace are allowed to pursue their goals, then men of violence would be given no quarter.

The British government's present policy in Northern Ireland perverts this order and provides frustration to the peacemakers and incentives to the violent. Just as surely as there is fire in the belly of the flint, there is disaster within such a policy. We must condemn violence as a solution, for it not only prolongs the agony in Ulster but diminishes each of us. Pope John Paul II warned that, in condoning or tolerating terrorist violence, "contemporary man is risking the death of his conscience."

The question then is not really why get involved in Northern Ireland's problems but, rather, how can we avoid doing so? We must galvanize American opinion by publicizing the facts of life in modern Ulster. We must bring pressure on whichever party is elected in Britain to take steps toward ending strife now and providing the basis for a settlement that will bring peace and justice to all the people of Northern Ireland within a defined timetable. The effort to heal the wounds between North and South will require the deft but strong touch of master surgeons. It will require delicate instruments in sure hands, but the patient can wait no longer.

The flames of bigotry still burn and the drums of ignorance still sound on the hills of Ulster. Futile and self-destructive violence continues; there has been obvious unwillingness in England to risk the votes of the past for peace in the future. For whatever reasons, the American media have also neglected the tragedy in Northern Ireland or reported it in only the most cursory manner. That neglect did not dissuade me, for tilting against the windmills of life was regular fare in the diet of my family.

The whole process of evolution behind *Irish Essays* may not be notably logical; it is, however, rather typically Irish. One story always reminds an Irishman of another and another. Only by presenting the myriad facets of Bloomsday did James Joyce capture the essence of his *Ulysses*. Gradually, different experiences begin to blend into a coherent image, a way of looking at the world, of interpreting life. It is hoped that the reader may discern such a coherence amid the diversity of these essays.

Threads for a Tapestry
1981

During an intense six year period of public service, when I directed New York State's health and human services departments, I delivered several hundred speeches,conceived and written in the heat of battle; they reflected the crises of the moment and were often geared to defend a particular policy or deflect an opposing argument. To accomplish this with philosophy, perspective, and a bit of poetry is the unique challenge that public speeches pose to a writer.

These are not leisurely essays, polished for publication; neither are they technical talks, replete with charts and statistics. Such details are obviously essential on some occasions, but that approach has already been provided in my book *Health in New York State* and in numerous articles and reports.

Rather, the speeches selected here are the spoken words of one who was privileged to fashion public policy and reflect my belief that the opportunity brought with it an obligation to articulate clearly the bases for difficult decisions. These talks offer an insight into my own approach to problems and demonstrate, I hope, some of the joy experienced while battling for a cause. They may also suggest that statements of public policy need not be framed in a bureaucratic patois which does violence to our language.

All in all, I suppose the arrangement of the speeches here will not satisfy the reader who demands a strict Aristotelian sense of order – with a beginning, a middle, and an end. It is more of a Joycean arrangement, with various speeches spun from different skeins but with the diverse strands woven into an emerging pattern. Art, it is said by some, imitates life, and each life is a tapestry of great complexity. Hopefully, the reader will be able to glimpse from these speeches – these threads – something of the wonder I find in the rich cloth of life.

As the title suggests, I see my own tapestry as obviously unfinished; in fact its final design seems blessedly unclear. The same threads may be woven into many different patterns, and possibly the best result of this whole book might be that some readers will use these same fibers to help create their own unique tapestry.

This period of public service ended in disillusionment. A politician with whom I had worked changed his methods of operation and in one morning I resigned from my multiple governmental positions. I concluded the book with the following parable:

Threads loosen and the patterns of the past unravel. Violence and neglect tear at the fabric of society, damaging the designs created by centuries of custom, shattering the dreams of those who find beauty and strength in the complex tapestry of life.

But the weaver cannot be discouraged merely because fools fail to appreciate tradition or deceive themselves by substituting colorful but weak fibers for the strong warp and weft of the craftsman's loom. The weaver's hands will not be stilled. With confidence he must continue interlacing yarns of different textures and hues. Experience teaches him to finish frazzled ends and preserve torn segments, to wind diverse strands into a coherent picture and, out of apparent chaos, create a new order.

The weaver is not alone, for he shares in the rich heritage of artisans who use time honored techniques to fashion the beautiful, protective cloth of life. While he must work within the confines of his loom, there are no other barriers to his imagination, and he can sew segments together for patterns of vast proportions. The weaver can bind the tears – the wounds – of a tapestry and shade his colors and tie his knots, producing a wondrous and lustrous reflection of the life he celebrates.

It's bad enough to be severely malnourished during a famine caused by war. Many of this young orphan's family had already died from intercurrent infections.

The boy had been dragged from his hut in the powerful jaws of marauding hyenas. He survived only because those terrible animals could not carry him away fast enough.

Throughout my professional life, I have balanced the rewards of being a physician in the center of New York City with an equally gratifying experience—intimate contact with the humbling essence of reality, caring for tropical patients in the poor and traumatized areas of the world.

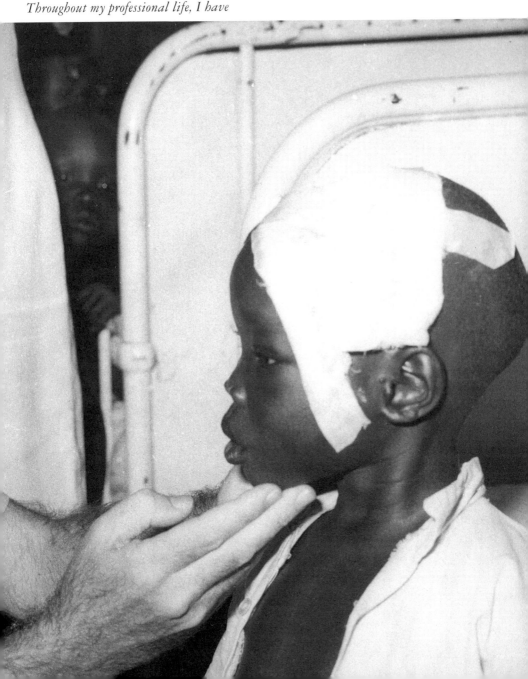

Famine
1982

Though blood may flow in both, there is a clear difference between a minor laceration and a hemorrhage. So, too, we must not confuse malnutrition or even hunger with famine. Famine is of a different scale, reflecting a prolonged total shortage of foods in a limited geographic area and leading to widespread disease and death from starvation.

Famines have occurred in all areas of the globe and in every period of recorded history. But the era in which we live has the odious distinction of being the period when more people will die of famine than in any previous century. To appreciate this indictment fully, it is necessary to review the traditional causes of famine and then to realize that today mass death by starvation is rarely due to the vagaries of nature but reflects, rather, human decisions. Today's famines are man made, for we have the ability to control short term food deficits.

Many factors can cause a local crop failure: droughts, floods, locusts, the spread of the desert, toxins, the erosion or exhaustion of soil. But in our modern world of instant communications and rapid transport, there must almost be a calculated effort for famine to flourish. There must be a failure of the social system and a denial of our obligation to share. Political decisions—or indecisions—ignorance, neglect, economic and cultural conflicts cause famine today.

Since we in the developed nations control the critical surplus food supplies of the world and have the capacity to both make and resolve or, as is too often the case, ignore famines, it is most appropriate that we reflect carefully on the history, reality, ethics, and response to famine. Eighty percent of the earth's population live in the developing nations of the Third World, where the specter of famine is ever present. It is for them—and for our children—that I write this book on famine.

The AIDS Epidemic
1983

Several years ago, healthy young men began to die in large numbers from an unknown disease. As so often happens in the history of medicine, the early cases were considered isolated extremes in the normal spectrum of any illness, and there was, in retrospect, an inadequate appreciation by the health professions of a growing disaster. Slowly, but inexorably, the numbers afflicted grew until this insidious disease exploded into a frightening epidemic.

Persons, who had been previously well, developed rare tumors and unusual systemic infections. Studies indicated that these patients had suddenly and inexplicably lost their normal immunity to disease. They had an illness for which modern medicine had no name and, in our ignorance, we called it Acquired Immune Deficiency Syndrome – or AIDS.

At first, most of the victims were homosexual men in New York City and California, but soon heterosexual Haitians and drug addicts were diagnosed. Then blood recipients, particularly hemophiliacs, fell before this new, puzzling, and deadly epidemic. Within eighteen months over a thousand cases were reported in the United States and Europe, with over five hundred in New York City.

There were many questions and few answers. Concern led to fear and mushroomed into panic. There were demands for drastic action, but no one was quite certain what to do. Federal officials seemed to approach the epidemic with embarrassment, declaring that the problem was a local issue; local authorities claimed they could do little without national support. Words and endless meetings became a substitute for rational action. Politicians handled the epidemic with unaccustomed wariness. Almost without exception, public leaders evaded the epidemic, avoiding even the usual expressions of compassion and concern. It was as if the sexual orientation of the victims made any involvement risky, and the politicians directed their courage and energies elsewhere.

Still the young men continued to die. But even as the disaster escalated, the organized medical community was strangely absent. When a fatal infection had struck down veterans attending an American Legion convention, health professionals across the country joined in the search for a solution. When women using tampons became ill with toxic shock syndrome, medical societies and research centers immediately focused their enormous talents on that problem. But when the victims were drug addicts and poor Haitian refugees and homosexual men, their plight did not, somehow, seem as significant to those expected to speak for the health professions. No major research programs were announced, and until it became clear that the disease could spread to the general population through blood transfusions, organized medicine seemed part of the curious conspiracy of silence.

Nevertheless, when historians reflect on this epidemic years hence, I suspect they will not stress the sordid stories of failure and neglect but rather recount the remarkable tales of heroism that illuminate this dark, lonely period of struggle to unravel the unknown. While government and organized medicine appeared to look for excuses for inaction, a new collective strength was building among those most at risk of contracting AIDS. Their greatest strength lay in a determination not to be destroyed, in a will that demanded public attention be paid to this epidemic and in an unprecedented willingness to help those who needed the medical, psychological, and social assistance that society had not offered. Out of such determination was formed the Gay Men's Health Crisis, a group that has done superb work educating, advising, and sustaining frightened, vulnerable people with nowhere else to turn.

No one has captured better than Albert Camus the unique exile an epidemic imposes. In *The Plague*, he wrote:

There was always something missing in their lives. Hostile to the past, impatient of the present, and cheated of the future, we were much like those whom men's justice, or hatred, forces to live behind prison bars... The plague had swallowed up everything and everyone. No longer were there individual destinies, only a collective destiny, made of plague and the emotions shared by all. Strongest of these emotions was the sense of exile and of deprivation, with all the cross currents of revolt and fear set up by these.

All too often, the victims of AIDS have been made to feel like Camus's victims, exiled and deprived of the full measure of what modern medicine can offer. But there have also been many instances of individual courage, of simple adherence by physicians and nurses and technicians to a code as old as medicine itself. These will never he recorded or acknowledged individually. Clinical medicine is not built on heroic deeds or memorable feats but on steady, loyal service to patients. When those patients are dying in large numbers and when the mode of transmission of their disease is unknown, then the daily routine of involved health workers assumes a quiet dignity and decency that deserves special respect.

The clinician has a privileged role in an epidemic, for he shares, uniquely, the victims' sufferings, their despair, and their dwindling hopes. In this epidemic, we, as physicians, have had daily to face patients in the prime of life who are suffering from a disease we do not understand and cannot cure. We have often had to sustain them solely with the ancient commitment of our profession to remain at our posts, seeking answers and offering help until this modern plague has been conquered.

Added to the medical challenge has been a growing crisis in hospitals and social service departments faced with large numbers of AIDS patients. Because of the need for isolation precautions, every facet of their care from nursing and nutrition to laboratory work and housekeeping becomes extremely costly. The duration of an AIDS hospital stay is usually measured in months, and hospital bills in excess of $100,000 occur with ever increasing frequency. Health insurance coverage for the young and poor, who constitute the majority of AIDS victims, is usually inadequate, often nonexistent. Society had not planned for this epidemic.

The history of medicine reassures us that, with time and effort, the terrible mystery of AIDS will be unraveled, and a cure found. I have no doubt that those whose words are presented here will have been major actors in bringing this life and death drama to an end.

When that day comes, we may look back and reflect with the same satisfaction that Camus's character, Dr. Rieux, experienced as the plague epidemic finally vanished from Oran:

And it was in the midst of shouts rolling against the terrace wall in massive waves that waxed in volume and duration, while cataracts of colored fire fell thicker through the darkness, that Dr. Rieux resolved to compile this chronicle, so that he should not be one of those who hold their peace but should bear witness in favor of those plague stricken people; so that some memorial of the injustice and outrage done them might endure; and to state quite simply what we learn in time of pestilence: that there are more things to admire in men than to despise.

A Bridge to Peace
1988

A bridge is a blend of poetry and practicality. By appreciating —and harnessing—tensions and forces man can span abysses, link separated lands, and create a thing of beauty. But soaring girders and graceful arches must be firmly anchored in a solid foundation, or even an expected load will cause collapse, destroying both bridge and travelers.

The imagery of a bridge seems appropriate for those who search for hope in a world where greed and arrogance abound. The prevalence of poverty and political oppression, hunger and disease, prejudice and ignorance can be denied only by the spiritually blind. Somehow the efforts to cross chasms of despair and join the disparate parts of a shattered earth must go beyond the physical. As we struggle against the forces of evil that continue to enslave the vast majority of humanity, we need lofty dreams, bridges of hope, to sustain our lonely steps.

Individual efforts are like a journey into emptiness. Only by forging common bonds can we conquer the gaps that divide us, and only mutual endeavors will build a community where peace, justice, and compassion can thrive. As a physician who has been privileged to share numerous crises with the peoples of the Third World, I have tried, with my writings, to capture the universal experiences of suffering and pain in order to express for my fellow citizens the terrible reality of life so often blurred by the obfuscations of politicians.

A Bridge to Peace was written over a five-year period (1982–87) when circumstances allowed me unusual entree into troubled communities around the world. It was written in the heat of battles and had to conform to the limited space permitted in newspaper editorial pages. Nevertheless, I hope the reader will find sufficient passion in the sparse style, for I record outrageous wrongs perpetrated in our name. Silence would have been almost as serious a sin as the acts of commission I condemn. And although these essays took unpopular positions, it required little courage to identify with those who suffer and die for freedom.

My reflections are based on a foundation of more than a quarter century of clinical and academic work in tropical medicine and in a philosophy that holds that health, and other humane endeavors, may well be the best – and sometimes the only – tools that can bridge differences and unite warring parties. The geographic distances encompassed within these essays emphasize how similar are the problems around the world and how a non violent bridge to peace can find application in all societies.

Imminent Peril
1991

The metaphors of the human body come naturally to a physician as he views the ills that plague modern society. Just like patients, cities can rot from within until nothing remains but a hulk artificially maintained by emergency infusions. The signs and symptoms of serious disease are usually obvious, in medical as well as political life except to those who wish to deny the evidence of steady deterioration and the possibility of death. To those who indulge in such folly, the healing arts offer no immunity. While diagnosis is often quite easy, devising and administering an appropriate treatment plan can be difficult for both doctor and patient. Cities and states have collapsed before because of benign neglect. Spasmodic efforts at revival are no substitute for a careful and even courageous course of therapy. It is important, at least for me in considering public health issues, to maintain that perspective.

We must remind ourselves that all the great city-states in the developed world were created by men and women who desired to live together, sacrificing the security of rural isolation for the stimulation of crowded, boisterous towns. Sometimes motivated by love, sometimes by greed, they conceived an urban structure that could sustain their dreams, wild dreams where trade, education, the arts, and political and religious freedoms would flourish in peace and harmony in an environment that depended upon safe supplies of shared water, food, and even air. Laws were passed to control pollution for the welfare, not only of the individual, but of the community at large. In every civilized society, the containment of infectious diseases took priority over commercial gain. The whole concept of quarantine (holding ships in the harbor for forty days) reflected the understanding and acceptance that the public's health stood above all else if a city was to thrive, or even survive.

In his observations on the system of democracy that flourished in this country in the early nineteenth century, Alexis de Tocqueville captured a characteristic American approach in the search for a healthy and safe environment. While emphasizing the individuality of our forebears, he noted their propensity to form civic organizations to guarantee fundamental rights. He wrote, "There is no end which the human will despairs of attaining by the free action of the collective power of individuals.... An association unites the energies of divergent minds and vigorously directs them toward a clearly indicated goal."

Today, there seems to be a steady diminution of that national spirit de Tocqueville so admired, a failure to see beyond immediate, selfish interests, a squandering of the unique heritage of America. The nation seems to have lost its bearings; our priorities have gone awry. Leaders must arrest this drift toward communal disintegration and personal self-destruction. For pragmatic as well as ethical reasons, I suggest this renewal begin with a political focus on public health.

Like de Tocqueville's early pioneers, we must begin our labors convinced that we can overcome the challenges of a harsh new world. I conceived *Imminent Peril* in the belief that even the most intractable problems in our country can be solved if only wise and determined citizens will become involved in helping to define, and then to strengthen, the necessary political course of action.

There are certainly ominous signs forecasting terrible times ahead for the health of our country unless there is a dramatic reorientation of governmental priorities. The world's premier public health system has been pushed toward extinction by draconian budget cuts. Across the land a demoralized professional core of public health workers are trying to cope with an unusual confluence of disparate forces, contending with the emergence of new and the resurgence of old communicable and fatal diseases. The AIDS crisis adds to the chaos by generating confusion, hysteria, and panic built, at least in part, on ignorance and fear. This ever-changing epidemic has accentuated the ancient clash between individual and public rights and best demonstrates our current, tragic paralysis in finding solutions at either level.

If we cannot test, if we cannot treat, if we cannot immunize, if we cannot educate, then we shall fall victim to a calamity that will not only fill the corridors of our hospitals but will soon cripple the economic engine and drive away those precious human resources that give life to cities such as New York. We simply cannot continue to replace reality with rhetoric.

The "public" served by the public health system is increasingly the disenfranchised, the uninsured, the impoverished, the homeless, the aged, the addicted. Failing their needs is more than morally indefensible in our new world order; it threatens the health of all. For as surely as an untreated tubercular lesion will cavitate the lungs of a homeless vagrant, so too will the deadly mist of his infection disseminate through every social and economic class, among innocent fellow riders in the subway, or passengers in an elevator and, inevitably, from child to child in the classrooms of our city.

Imminent Peril offers historical, legal, and field reports that should challenge America's soul. This present crisis must teach us, once again and maybe forever, that no one – no individual, no family, no city, state, or nation – can hope to reach its potential as long as so many are denied their basic rights to public health protection.

Public health programs are not political privileges to be parceled out annually. They must be recognized as fundamental, nonnegotiable prerogatives of every citizen. Such public services must be held immune from those who measure value merely with fiscal scales. There are irreducible levels of health care and prevention that are absolute requirements in the rare system of government our Founding Fathers created.

With an optimism that is necessary to sustain those of us who are privileged to spend our lives amidst dreams as well as sufferings, I conclude *Imminent Peril* with a section on "New Approaches," unabashedly trying to promote a characteristic that de Tocqueville saw as the essence of America—the willingness to face difficulties together, to make of adversity an opportunity for new thinking, new ways of acting. And if we do it correctly, perhaps we can entice the entire nation, and all its leaders, back to the vision that the good health and welfare of the public is the very foundation of our society. If we were to truly understand this, then never again would public health budgets be gutted, and our efforts would be worthwhile indeed. The hour for the rebirth of a caring and compassionate country is here. This is a time to renew old priorities that may still allow urban society—with all its failings—to become the mythical "city on the hill" of our dreams.

A Framework for Survival
1999

In a world where chaos and conflict are endemic, at a time when violence and votes are sweeping away the political contours we once thought permanent, in countries battered by economic collapse and internecine wars, when great nations are disintegrating into unworkable ethnic enclaves, and survival seems secure only in clan structures, when hatred and massacres, hunger, and epidemics run rampant, there is, nonetheless, a glimmer of hope in the growing recognition that, for better or worse, we are all neighbors on a finite globe, and that the oppression and starvation and illnesses of others are ultimately our own.

We live in an era when the very foundations of civilized society are shifting or collapsing. National sovereignty is no longer accepted as an absolute right or as a shield from inquiry into local oppression. Rather than being protected in times of conflict, women and children have now become primary targets in avenging ancient hatreds, and the victims of violence that is justified by grossly misreading the lessons of religion and history. Instant communications make human rights violations and widespread physical suffering matters of personal concern; they can never again be relegated to the shadows of our minds, for now willful inaction makes us participants in crimes against humanity.

It is impossible to hide today from even distant catastrophes. Bloated bellies and destroyed societies are no longer only sad stories to be debated by statesmen far removed in time and space from the carnage. Now the images are on our television screens; they are a major force in our own and our children's continuous education. Unless we intend to give up being human, we can no longer feel warm and secure in our homes while disasters swirl through the cold world outside.

The fact that we know, instantly and vividly, that terrible wrongs are occurring creates a moral and legal burden that did not weigh on previous generations. We cannot simply talk about problems, deceiving ourselves that words—even heartfelt concerns—can substitute for corrective actions and compassionate deeds. Time is not on the side of those who believe that we can maintain the status quo, that we can continue to confront reality with old rhetoric and allow the past to happen over and over again.

Many recent crises clearly demonstrate why humanitarian issues should be absolutely central in America's foreign policy. These issues are usually considered—if they are considered at all—as peripheral concerns by those who formulate and implement our overseas agendas. Yet I offer the following examples:

1. When Ebola breaks out in the Congo or plague erupts in India, the old logic of quarantine is now irrelevant. The speed of travel and the mass movement of people have destroyed any assurance of isolation from, or protection against, the spread of deadly diseases. Epidemics can threaten our basic security as surely as nuclear weapons, yet the imbalance in government spending is appalling. In recent foreign aid bills, forty times more dollars are allocated for military aid to other nations than are set aside for all foreign disaster assistance.

2. Consider the impact of HIV infection and AIDS in Africa.

Are these purely medical concerns? *The Washington Post* wrote an editorial about a preliminary study documenting that more than fifty percent of the armed forces in seven African nations are HIV positive. This is not a surprising figure when you consider that soldiers are young, relatively wealthy, mobile, and have a tradition of imposing their will along the highways and chaotic areas that characterize so much of turbulent Africa. But if you simultaneously consider that the very stability of most African states is predicated, for better or worse, on the military, then you must conclude that the foundation of these nations is fragile indeed, resting on a group of very sick people with a short life expectancy in areas where diagnostic facilities and effective medications for AIDS are simply not available. The average annual health budget in many poor African countries is between $5 and $10 per capita, while the cost for antiviral drugs alone can exceed $10,000 per person per year.

3. To further complicate the African AIDS disaster and to emphasize the diplomatic implications of health issues, it should be noted that there are no pre-employment HIV tests when the United Nations deploys armed divisions from endemic zones to be part of their Blue Beret forces. Therefore, troops dedicated to peacekeeping are undoubtedly simultaneously contributing to the dissemination of fatal infections.

We must devise innovative methods and better diagnostic, therapeutic, and preventive techniques to deal with such challenges. If we fail, already existent problems will multiply just as surely as a microbe flourishes in fertile ground. We no longer have the luxury of ignoring humanitarian crises for, even viewed selfishly, we know they have the potential to destroy our own and our children's lives. One would have to be blind, or arrogant, or very foolish to ignore so many obvious disasters in waiting.

The number and severity of humanitarian crises is rapidly escalating in our post Cold War era, where the perverse stability of East-West superpower politics can sometimes seem preferable to the chaos that now prevails in "failed states" that dot the world. Civil wars have largely replaced formal conflicts between nations. International humanitarian laws, which were established to provide rules of war, are rarely recognized and are surely not observed in civil wars. International laws and Geneva Conventions were composed for an earlier era when state governments officially represented combatants. Now, childhood warriors with AK47s rule the roads, and clans use ethnic cleansing as a solution to borders that, according to one's own peculiar view, had been artificially imposed by a historical process they would never forget nor forgive. Today, there are more internally displaced persons than international refugees.

In noncomplex emergencies such as floods or earthquakes, where a stable government does exist, it is responsible for (and understandably expects to handle) all relief activities. International assistance workers must accept the traditions and rules of functioning sovereign nations or invite confrontation and painful rejection. Aid offered without respect for the rights of an independent people will almost always result in counterproductive misunderstanding, damaging both donor and recipient.

But in complex humanitarian emergencies, security concerns and political decisions are an intimate part of any relief response. Complex humanitarian emergencies are characterized by the total disruption or destruction of the existing public infrastructure, leading to a situation where there is often no accepted government and usually no functioning health, transportation, police, or welfare systems. There is, therefore, no recourse for those caught in the cross fires of war or chaos, nor for international humanitarian workers willing, but often unable, to help. There is usually nowhere to hide, and those who must stay are the most vulnerable—women, children, and the elderly. Humanitarian assistance workers are no longer seen by hostile communities as respected and protected neutral healers; increasingly they become the hostages and victims of an anarchy they cannot control.

So we enter an era when humanitarian assistance—whether provided by international agencies such as the United Nations or the Red Cross, by governments, or by local and international voluntary agencies—can no longer be delivered using accepted ground rules by which earlier generations could play. The foundations of many societies are eroding, and the bases for a new structure of nations have yet to emerge. Furthermore, the aid community and its donors have also lost their innocence and realize that they must carefully assess and question what good humanitarian projects do.

Everyone who tries to offer help in the midst of conflicts and disasters is now painfully aware of the dangers of external aid, of staying too long, and of even feeding hungry societies. Surplus foods may seriously damage the traditional farming and herding patterns that had sustained indigenous populations through all their previous calamities of drought and conflict. The world has learned the horrifying lesson that inappropriate humanitarian aid often becomes a tool of destruction.

Concern for innocent victims of war and soul wrenching images of stricken women and children are the rationales most frequently invoked in justifying international intervention in areas of conflict and disaster. Then, as if it were a predetermined role, statesmen and soldiers, lawyers and economists, politicians and academicians, invariably formulate foreign policies and offer solutions that are often more relevant to their own interests and cultural sensibilities than to the realities of the situations they seek to address. Their efforts seem, with incredible regularity, to provoke a recurrent cycle of tragedies. Rarely do these leaders seek the views of, or benefit from the experiences of, those who must deal with the terrible carnage that inevitably follows military maneuvers or natural catastrophes.

Health workers know most intimately the pain and waste of battle. They also have the privilege of healing wounds and relieving the pangs of starvation; occasionally, and uniquely, they can secure the trust and cooperation of adversaries. Their role in conflict resolution offers an innovative direction in a global diplomacy searching for new approaches.

International humanitarian assistance has never been a simple undertaking. I recall my first experiences in Somalia in 1963; a newly independent nation was being decimated by an unknown disease. In some towns over 10 percent of the population had died from a fulminant diarrhea, and bodies littered the countryside. Even then—over forty years ago and despite all the enthusiasm of youth—one quickly came to understand how artificial it was to think that if we identified the biological cause and defined the appropriate therapy, the epidemic would be solved. It was also difficult to pretend that our efforts were purely impartial and altruistic; I was directing an American military research group and reporting to the local U.S. ambassador. Even if I didn't fully fathom the relationships, I knew politics played a role in our assignment. And one quickly learned that foreign interventions were not always selfless or even beneficial.

Obviously, there was great satisfaction in alleviating suffering in a nation of nomads with few doctors, fewer than twenty miles of paved roads and minimal government structures. Flexibility and adaptation were essential, and humility came quickly. Those first experiences in large-scale humanitarian relief projects introduced me to the politics of aid and the necessity for logistics and other disciplines that were not taught in medical school. I became acutely aware of the impact of new foods and medicines and money in a traditional society that, to our dismay, quickly learned to abuse them all.

I kept a research team in Somalia for the next thirty five years, shared in their good days and bad, and directed refugee programs during the early 1980s when one and a half million starving victims of drought required aid. And yet, when most of the modern world thinks of Somalia today, they conjure up images of only the bloated bellies and cachectic faces seen on TV during the famine in the early 1990s, of civil war, of peacekeepers killed, of aid organizations fleeing to the safety of neighboring countries. The lessons of previous aid efforts seemed to be utterly forgotten in a multibillion, unfocused extravaganza that soon matched the surrounding chaos and wastefulness.

As the basic structures of government and society on the Horn of Africa fell under the weight of corruption and greed, humanitarian workers faced fundamental challenges and had to make radical changes. Even the best intentioned and most experienced aid organizations modified their principles in order to survive. They hired armed thugs to protect themselves against other armed thugs. Unwittingly they had become, because of their food and vehicles and money, major actors in the tragedy that is still unraveling in Somalia.

By the early 1990s, international aid was the largest portion of the Somali national budget and propped up a corrupt and repressive regime. When Mohammed Siad Barre's government collapsed, and national starvation reached critical proportions, many humanitarian organizations did not acquit themselves with great honor. United Nations agencies worked from the safety of Kenya, and voluntary organizations overtly used the crisis to raise their own fundraising profile. Nations such as the United States found an easy way to unload enormous amounts of surplus food and reinforce a tragic cycle of dependence.

The same tale can be told in the Great Lakes region of Central Africa. With the benefit of hindsight, everyone now recognizes that maintaining the camps of Hutu refugees after the Rwanda genocide merely perpetuated the hold of killers and prolonged the agony of the innocent. In Bosnia, humanitarian and human rights workers were caught in the unenviable position of knowing that pursuing their principles and maintaining relief efforts were helping – not hindering – the pace of ethnic cleansing.

Yet, out of these disasters much good has come. For the international humanitarian community began to assess honestly its approach and to question openly its methods as well as its motives. The world had changed utterly in the rubble of Mogadishu. The innocence of the sixties and seventies had vanished.

The foreign policy of any nation reflects its fears and dreams, as well as its own particular political and economic interests. In the Cold War era, convinced that our national security was under constant mortal threat, the United States allowed the element of fear to become dominant. Our overseas agenda failed to take into account that the growing disparities between rich and poor, hungry and nourished, free and oppressed had become the driving forces in conflicts around the world.

Now, as the only remaining superpower and finally freed from our Cold War fears, we can afford to be compassionate as well as strong and, by emphasizing health and humanitarian assistance, we could fashion a foreign policy capable of rekindling an American spirit that is now being strangled at home and abroad. The relationship of health, human rights and humanitarian assistance to foreign policy is not a theoretical exercise. Today, most foreign interventions by the United States are predicated, or at least defended, on humanitarian bases: starving Somalis, homeless Kurds, dead Rwandans. Yet, in my experience, few political or diplomatic leaders understand the health and humanitarian issues they so readily invoke.

162

By building on common objectives and universally accepted values, by defining the core needs of all human beings, and by proposing ways to satisfy those needs, we may be able to create a better framework for survival in a new century. Focusing on health, human rights and humanitarian assistance offers an innovative approach to foreign policy that may be more effective in many cases than the conventional military, economic, and geopolitical "solutions" that have so often been so flawed.

Humanitarian workers can open doors and establish corridors but still have little or no impact on the prevention or resolution of conflicts. To change the perceptions of responsibility, the traditional prerogatives of actors in a political process, is not easy and comes slowly. Politicians usually consider humanitarian workers as do-gooders who are presumed to be too innocent to understand the harsh realities of diplomatic decision making. Health, human rights, and humanitarian assistance concerns are usually invoked to justify interventions, and relief workers are praised, particularly if the media can record a nation's compassion, and then they are dismissed. In the past, relief workers accepted as an adequate reward the instant and enormous gratification that comes in healing the wounds of war without demanding any further involvement, without, in most circumstances, even staying long enough to assess critically their own efforts.

For example, humanitarian workers have long embraced the comforting concept of neutrality, without carefully weighing its political implications. In World War II, few seemed seriously to question whether the Red Cross was morally right to distribute biscuits and food parcels in Auschwitz or Buchenwald but never criticize or publicly condemn Nazi extermination methods. Do today's humanitarian workers have the courage to question whether the aid they deliver is used to foster oppression as a tool for ethnic cleansing? Do we merely prolong the agonies of war when we contribute supplies without weighing whether our help may simultaneously perpetuate the genocidal power of evil leaders, as happened in the Goma refugee camps? Is it ever possible to stay professionally aloof from such practical, political, and deeply moral questions, especially ones that are both predictable and inevitable?

Humanitarian assistance in international conflicts always

has a political dimension. This should not be a source for embarrassment; it is a simple fact of life. Politics affects everyone in the chain—from the donors, to the distributors, to the recipients. One has only to look at the funding of large voluntary agencies in the United States to appreciate the political dimension. The Cooperative for Assistance and Relief Everywhere (CARE), for example, seen as the compassionate voluntary effort of concerned American individuals, receives the vast amount of its budget from the United States Agency for International Development (USAID) and other government sources—and the person who pays the piper can surely call the tune. Decisions about who gets food, when, and for how long are based on political factors.

America's multimillion dollar effort to assist oppressed Kurds in Northern Iraq, code named *Operation Provide Comfort*, was canceled within a week when our favored Kurdish faction decided they were safer with local Iraqi, rather than our preferred Iranian, protection. The cover of humanitarian concern was blown away by the cold winds of political reality. I was in Somalia when President Bush sent in 35,000 troops to help the starving masses. TV cameras and reporters were flown to Mogadishu in advance so they could record the troop landings for the evening television news/entertainment. One year and $4 billion later, we left a country in chaos.

One can seriously argue what good, if any, came from the whole sad experience. Anarchy still reigns in Somalia, but the attention of a fickle world, overwhelmed by other tragedies, has moved on. Somalia is no longer newsworthy. Political judgments dictated our arrival and departure schedules. The knowledge or insights of academics and health workers who knew the people and the customs of the Somalis seemed to matter very little to those who defined our national interest.

The United States had entered Somalia because of a putative concern about the health of a starving populace. The foreign policy results of a noble gesture gone awry were far more profound than the scenes of famine we were supposed to eliminate. As with Vietnam, a great tragedy flowed from our failed involvement in Somalia. America's relationship with the United Nations unraveled, with catastrophic implications for future international humanitarian missions.

When civil unrest in Rwanda erupted in 1994, UN Secretary-General Boutros Boutros Ghali literally begged the Security Council to send an expanded peacekeeping force. The United States led the opposition to this appeal because we did not wish to cross what was now called the "Mogadishu line," the commitment of American forces under a UN flag in a foreign country. Within the next two months, 800,000 Rwandans were hacked to death with machetes, and the churches and lakes were clogged with the corpses of innocent victims of neglect. We knew what was happening, and we watched but did little except debate procedures, arguing over the methods of payment for surplus transport that had to be assured before we would become involved.

Fifty years after the Holocaust, after our nation joined in the chorus of "never again," we silently observed the most intense months of genocide in the history of mankind. Then the most massive movement of refugees in world history began; in a single day more than a million people poured into the small town of Goma in eastern Zaire (Congo). Very late in the course of the disaster, the same donor governments that had refused to help months before now poured $2 billion into an uncoordinated relief effort that resulted in sustaining the very murderers we had failed to stop when the genocide began.

So the question "How can we help?" is usually asked too late, and those who wish to respond are often inadequately prepared for the tasks they must face. Many well-intentioned individuals, and organizations who want to help lack the requisite skills to intervene and the expertise to know which interventions are likely to be effective. There is an urgent need for an internationally recognized basic minimum standard of training for personnel involved in humanitarian assistance.

Humanitarian projects can offer the common ground necessary to initiate dialogue between combatants who might agree on little else. Vaccination programs have allowed "corridors of tranquility," de facto cease fire zones, to be established in the midst of bitter wars. As I have witnessed in the Sudan, Nicaragua, and Lebanon, among other conflict zones, humanitarian projects can sometimes serve as the only acceptable bridges to peace; they offer an opening wedge, and we must learn to utilize and develop this untapped resource.

Those of us privileged to participate in great humanitarian dramas have the opportunity adversity offers to build a new framework, using – and sometimes rediscovering – the best of the old structures, but realizing that a new spirit and innovative methods are necessary for international discourse in a new millennium. Our success – or failure – will, to a large extent, define the chances for the very survival of the world.

There are no final answers; there cannot be in our finite and imperfect state. In public health, all the old challenges remain, and new diseases seem constantly to emerge. The explosion of drug resistant tuberculosis is a classic result of public complacency about a resurgent, infectious plague; new viruses and environmental changes continue to challenge our capacity to adapt and respond. So, too, in the endless search for world peace, statesmen realize that one cannot afford simply to accept failure, to adhere impotently to outmoded approaches. None should be surprised that our noble goals prove elusive, and we must constantly adapt if we are to survive.

Ultimately, that is my basis for hope. I am convinced that, despite all our failures, we can, by cooperating in efforts to heal the wounds of war and eliminate the causes of widespread spread violence, construct a new framework to support society's endless search for peace.

I first became interested in landmine victims in the midst of the Contra-Sandinista War in Nicaragua when legless patients would stare at me with hopeless and understandable anger. The same accusing gazes were even more numerous in my annual visits to northern Somalia where there were few hospital beds and no amputee programs. Sophisticated prostheses were simply too costly and required trained surgeons and rehabilitation technicians, specialists either unavailable or already overwhelmed by the demands of those who were thought to be salvageable. Triage can be a cruel exercise.

The existence of a very inexpensive, mass-produced, easily-fitted prosthesis changed our approach. This young Somali girl was the first double amputee I fitted with "Jaipur" feet.

For almost two years after she had lost her limbs to a hidden landmine, she moved by crawling like a crab. Within a day of being fitted with these below-the-knee, twelve dollar, polyurethane prostheses, she could walk. A year later, she was chosen to go to a UN conference on landmines in Geneva, Switzerland. As she walked across the stage to be photographed with the UN Secretary-General, she, who had never seen a building over one story high, had never been on an airplane or in a hotel, had never seen snow or an auditorium full of clapping diplomats, froze in panic. Then she recognized me in the audience and ran from the stage into my protective arms, crying in Somali, "Daddy, Daddy." Experiences like that make all the hard, lonely, and often frustrating field work worthwhile.

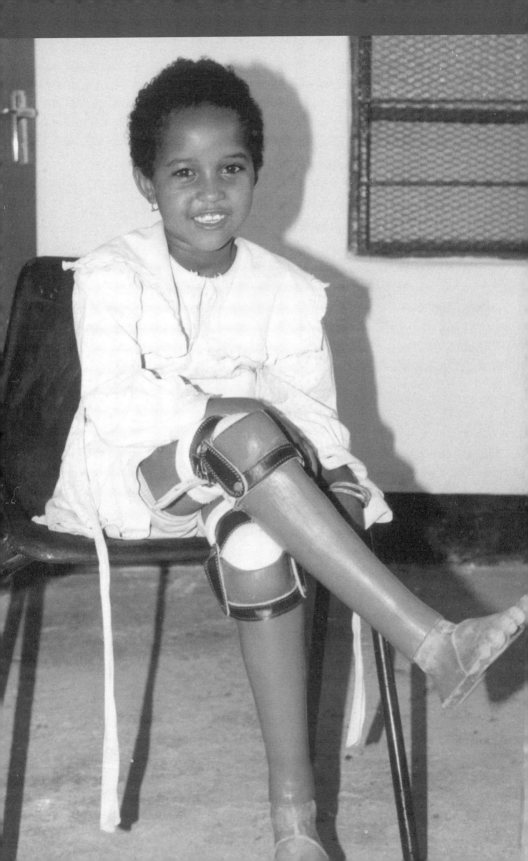

Clearing the Fields
1995

In the fertile grazing grounds of Somaliland, mothers now tie toddlers to trees so that the young children cannot crawl, innocently but dangerously, out among the more than one million mines that have been haphazardly laid there over the last decade. Camels, and the youngsters and adolescents who tend them, are less fortunate, since, to survive in the Somali savannah, animals must endlessly search for water and nourishment. The fields are littered with animal carcasses, and stone mounds mark the graves of herders. The towns are crowded with amputees. Mine injuries have become one of the major health hazards in that sad country, reaching epidemic proportions in the north.

Numerous international conferences, Congressional and United Nations hearings, and extensive media coverage have heightened our awareness of the growing problems posed by landmines. These efforts have documented the horror of mine injuries and the vast—indeed global—scope of the crisis. The educational process, however, has almost become an end in itself, with articles repeating articles, using the same data in an orgy of condemnations. But the emphasis has rarely, if ever, been on possible solutions. One has been expected to find solace merely in continuing to express outrage. However, the growing number of mine victims demands, if nothing else, that we move beyond rhetoric, beyond merely reconstructing limbs, to stop the spread of a devastating epidemic and devise a permanent cure.

Physicians know, perhaps better than most, that no words can mask the human suffering that war inevitably brings. I have seen the landmine crisis firsthand as a physician. In directing medical and public health programs in Nicaragua and Somalia, I have had to deal with the mutilated bodies; the crippled and blinded; the psychologically traumatized; and the devastating effects on families, communities, regions, and countries. But a physician's view is not merely medical; he does not cease to be an involved citizen merely because he wears a stethoscope or uses a scalpel. In fact, those experienced and skilled in international health can offer unique insights, and even solutions, not usually found in foreign policy debates, legal formulations, or military lore.

The special evil of antipersonnel landmines is that they do not discriminate between the civilian and the soldier, and they continue to maim and kill innocent victims long after the conflict in which they were deployed is over. But that is neither the beginning nor the end of the problem. Landmines are considered by military establishments to be indispensable defensive weapons in interstate warfare; they have also become offensive weapons of choice in internal conflicts, as can be seen in many Third World countries. Additionally, they are easy to make, profitable to sell, and relatively inexpensive to acquire.

Mines no longer have to be laid individually but can be scattered over vast areas, dropped from airplanes or delivered by rockets. It is virtually impossible to map the location of mines delivered by such "sophisticated" systems. Both sides employ mines in war, but media interpretation and official condemnation are the prerogatives only of the victor. In the Persian Gulf War, for example, much attention was devoted to the minefields Iraq laid inside Kuwait. However, little notice was given to the millions of mines rocketed by the allied forces deep into Iraq, far from the battlefields—one mine for every Iraqi man, woman, and child.

The constant development and refinement of the instruments of war has been the most malignant result of the technological revolution of our times. Public protest has rightly been aroused, and international action taken, against the threat of biological, chemical, and nuclear weapons. Landmines do not just pose a threat; they blow up innocent people every hour of everyday. It is time to consider whether they, too, should be deemed a particularly inhumane weapon that should be circumscribed by international law.

Landmines are one of the great scourges of history. They are turning vast areas of the earth into wastelands of death, economic ruin, and social disintegration. More than 100 million landmines are now scattered wantonly across the fields, roads, and other strategic areas of some 60 countries. Up to 30 million mines have been laid in Africa. In the Middle East, mines used during the Iran-Iraq and Persian Gulf wars have been added to those still lying in wait from World War II. Since 1990, an estimated 3 million mines have been sown, without markers or maps, among embattled civilians in the former Yugoslavia, and the total there is growing by some 50,000 per week.

Part of the problem is the sheer number of mines, and of the manufacturers and exporters of them. More than 250 million landmines, including approximately 200 million antipersonnel landmines, have been produced over the past twenty-five years. Antipersonnel landmines continue to be made at an average rate of 5–10 million per year. Approximately fifty nations produce these weapons, and about thirty export them. With such widespread distribution, no one escapes; in the recent Somali conflict, 26 percent of U.S. casualties were due to inexpensive, low technology, easy-to-use, conventional landmines–the same mines that are currently contaminating so much of the developing world.

Landmines are now used to terrorize and disrupt whole populations, not simply to block or control battlefield movements, as during World War II. The very concept of a "battlefield" that can be demarcated in space and time is, in fact, no longer valid. The entire countryside is now fair game in most conflicts, and the hapless inhabitants become part of every conflict. In World War I, only 5 percent of those killed or wounded were noncombatants; by World War II, the level was 50 percent, and the figure has approached 90 percent in recent conflicts. Defending the use of landmines by invoking obsolete battlefield definitions and military logic offers a seriously flawed argument in which unchallenged language distorts reality.

Long after armies leave, long after cease fires and even peace treaties have been signed, still hidden mines continue to do their terrible work on a devastating scale, especially in the twenty most ravaged countries, from Cambodia, Afghanistan, and Vietnam to Angola, Mozambique, and Somalia; from El Salvador and Nicaragua to Iraq and Kuwait. Because of the presence or fear of landmines, almost half the land area of Cambodia is unsafe for farming or any other human use. After eighteen years of civil war and 2 million landmines, no major road in Mozambique is usable. In Angola, the loss of arable land is so massive that the World Food Programme had to earmark $32 million of its 1994 food aid budget merely to offset nutritional deficiencies.

Refugees are afraid to return to their homes, creating a growing financial burden on international relief agencies. Landmines have cut the expected rate of repatriation in Cambodia from 10,000 to 1,000 per week. In Afghanistan the situation is even worse. Some 3.5 million refugees will not return because mountain roads and fields are infested with mines. The bill for refugees refusing to leave the camps in Pakistan was $50 million in 1993. In southern Sudan, mines have paralyzed agricultural production, leaving thousands trapped in a drought-stricken region. Everywhere, power plants, transportation centers, water supplies, and other essential services are primary mining targets so that the basic infrastructure of society collapses, and economic independence becomes a painful mirage.

In landmine infested areas, medical and public health teams are overwhelmed; the problems of evacuation, triage, and surgical treatment are daunting, but the challenges of rehabilitation are staggering. While over 1,000 people are killed by mines every month, many more are injured and permanently disabled. In Cambodia, one in every 236 people is a landmine amputee; the rate is one in 470 in Angola, and one in 1,000 in northern Somalia. One of the most significant, and most neglected, features of landmines is that the cost of clearing a minefield is at least 100 times that of laying it; in addition, clearance is a highly dangerous and painfully slow process. The number of deminers killed in Kuwait since the Persian Gulf War exceeds that of U.S. combatants killed during the conflict.

The enormity of the global landmine crisis and the increasing rage against the special crimes that mines commit against the innocent, in times of peace as well as conflict, are finally and belatedly generating public demands for action. But what action? What can be done?

One might view the landmine crisis in the same way as the ruler in *The King and I* saw the confusing challenges of change—as a "puzzlement" that no single approach and no single actor can solve. Certainly, no amount of ranting will help any longer, and a piecemeal approach is obviously inadequate for the growing disaster.

Yet, the problem was created by man's ingenuity—perverse, to be sure—and ultimately will have to be solved by the combined, cooperative, and coordinated efforts of many people.

The solutions will depend on technical and military experts with creative technological ideas. They will depend on lawyers who are willing to grapple with the elusive and frustrating verbal nuances that must be overcome if new, enforceable conventions, regimes, and agreements are to be fashioned. They will depend on doctors and humanitarian workers who can create models that may solve some of the most pressing problems posed by landmine injuries. And they will depend on diplomats and politicians who are willing to move beyond the boundaries of Cold War power politics to forge new treaties and provide innovative leadership, rather than merely repeat the slogans of the past. Solutions are possible.

Civilian and military approaches to the landmine crisis need not be mutually exclusive; in fact, the primary function of the United States military is to protect the safety of our citizens and to do so, ultimately, under civilian command. For philosophical as well as practical reasons, the military must play an essential role in solving the landmine crisis.

Responsible military leaders share the ethical concerns about landmines and must balance the transient benefits these weapons offer against their overwhelming impact on noncombatants and the social and economic price they impose on fragile nations. Only the military currently possesses the information, expertise, and organization that could reverse the landmine crisis. If the military were directed to share their knowledge and skills with civilian forces in a global demining program, immediate progress could be anticipated.

Much of the technology needed to mount an effective demining operation already exists, but the necessary political will and financial commitment have been wanting. International humanitarian law and conventions could easily be strengthened, but, once again, such change demands a political determination that has been sadly lacking. Surgical and public health programs for landmine victims could be standardized, thereby making them more economical and accessible in poorer countries where the burden is greatest. If we are not to perpetuate the present haphazard response system, in which flawed programs are repeatedly launched in different parts of the world, international coordination and cooperation are required. The United Nations Department of Humanitarian Affairs should be designated and funded to undertake this task.

Clearing the Fields is the effort of men and women, in and out of government, representing different disciplines and ideologies, all searching for solutions to a universally recognized disaster. Rooted firmly in the hard reality of their experiences, the contributors to this volume document the crisis and then explore possible avenues of escape. There is an almost palpable feeling that solutions to the landmine crisis can be realized, even if political leaders must be forced to follow the will of an aroused populace.

Hope rests on a worldwide movement, a slow, stumbling coalescence of determined private groups influencing governments and international organizations, even if each is motivated by different reasons. There is growing revulsion at the waste of innocent life, at the fear and despair that permeate mine infested lands, and at the skyrocketing costs to donor and recipient nations alike. There is a reluctant acceptance that current military methods can be changed, if necessary, and that the required technological and legal tools for resolving the crisis are already available or could be developed. Finally, the bright light of public scrutiny has exposed the lack of political thought and leadership on this topic. The hour has come at last; solutions to the landmine crisis are at hand.

Preventive Diplomacy
2000

One of the supreme creations of the human spirit is the idea of prevention. Like liberty and equality, it is a seminal concept drawn from a reservoir of optimism that centuries of epidemics, famines, and wars have failed to deplete. It is an amalgam of hope and possibility which assumes that misery is not an undefiable mandate of fate, a punishment only redeemable in a later life, but a condition that can be treated like a disease and sometimes cured or even prevented.

During a lifetime in the practice of medicine—in Africa, Latin America, and Asia, as well as my own country—I have seen the daily wonders of the healing arts: lives rescued from once fatal cancers, epidemics miraculously cut short; and countless millions of people saved from communicable diseases like polio and smallpox. Indeed, the conquest of smallpox, one of history's deadliest scourges, is itself a triumph of prevention attributable not only to Edward Jenner's vaccine but to the skills and untiring efforts of thousands of public health workers over a span of two hundred years.

So it is only natural for me to think of clinical and public health models in contemplating the disorders now threatening the health of the world community as it emerges from the rigid alignments of the Cold War and gropes for a new organizing principle in a new age of high technology, global economic competition, and multipolar politics. For power balances, realpolitik, and the other blunt-edged tools of East-West confrontation simply do not fit the need now for far more subtle, creative, and prospective approaches to the problems of peace.

The awesome challenges that face us are quite different from the nation-state rivalries and alliances that preoccupied statesmen during the previous century. They call for earlier diagnoses and new kinds of therapy. Underlying causes have to be attacked sooner rather than later, before they become fulminating infections that rage beyond rational control or political containment.

This, the defining principle of preventive diplomacy, argues that social detection and early intervention should be as honored in international relations as crisis management and political negotiation. In its pristine form, the idea is simplicity itself; it is reason opposed to irrationality, peace preferred to violence. In the reality of a disorderly world, however, preventive diplomacy is incredibly more complex and, in some respects, controversial. People can disagree on how to define social health and political disease. The tensions between rights and obligations seem to be intractable. Conflict is often needed to achieve social progress, so it is not always and forever to be shunned. In cases of unrelieved injustice, even violence may be justified. The challenges and hopes for preventive diplomacy are based on the conviction that it will contribute to the emergence of a more benign international system that can reduce the violence and suffering that now blight the lives of far too many millions of our fellow human beings.

The very breadth of this view of preventive diplomacy suggests that the term is far more restrictive than its purpose and conception. For diplomacy, as it has been practiced during most of a now dying Industrial Age, has been centered on the idea of nation-states dealing with each other on a government-to-government basis with the help of professionals specializing in secret negotiations and political conspiracy. Now, however, international relations have been utterly transformed by the technological revolution, by better-informed and more active publics, by the spread of market capitalism, the fragmentation of politics, and a veritable explosion of commercial transactions and nongovernmental activism. Even the supposedly bedrock principle of national sovereignty is being eroded.

The sources of human stress, community breakdown, and group violence are far too diverse and too deeply embedded in social change to be consigned to the windowless compartments of conventional diplomacy. Many problems do not move in a straight line but in endless gyres of cause and effect so that a fall in coffee prices, for example, triggers economic collapse in Rwanda, then enormous personal hardships followed by social unrest, genocide, and fleeing refugees, starvation, cholera, dysentery, and other diseases that overwhelm medical workers and relief organizations. The cycle of disaster involves many different disciplines, including medicine, so that prevention calls for a symphony rather than a solo performance by a single profession like diplomacy. It also calls for a new kind of diplomat. Preventing conflict requires different skills from resolving conflict, even though they cannot always be separated out. Yet diplomats, unlike physicians, have not fully developed a preventive ethos and a disciplined method of working.

I have long suggested that health and humanitarian issues should be the pragmatic as well as the symbolic centerpiece of American foreign policy and that the methodology of public health, and even the universally understood semantics of medicine, provide an exceptionally solid basis for a new type of diplomacy. But if preventive diplomacy is to replace traditional reactive diplomacy, there must be fundamental change in our national mind set. At present, only problems that attain crisis proportion seem to attract the attention of politicians or diplomats. Our leaders simply are not attuned to incipient disorders at a time when prevention is possible.

Public figures are obsessed with dramatic solutions, with a fire brigade approach that assures a continuation of catastrophes. In preventive medicine one begins by searching for fundamental causes, for the etiology of a disease, and for techniques that can interrupt transmission before serious signs and symptoms become obvious and irreversible damage occurs.

The origins of violence clearly lie in incubating prejudices and injustices that inevitably breed hatred and conflict. But how rarely are these evil forces exposed early enough, or fought with effective tools, before predictable disaster strikes? If a fatal disease threatens to spread, health experts devise control programs based on careful research and laboratory experiments. When deaths do occur, scrupulous postmortem analyses are customary, so that the errors and failures of the past become the building blocks for a better approach in the future. Diplomatic exercises should be subjected to similar probes and autopsies. Nations, particularly great powers and international organizations, must become humble enough to learn from failed efforts rather than merely defend traditional practices. If there are new actors in world conflicts and a new global environment created by, among other factors, a communications revolution, then the therapeutics of international mediation must also change.

The international system is in transition so that the contours of the post-Cold War age are still far from clear. But already there are a number of fascinating trends that are central to the development of the preventive diplomacy idea. One is a tentative shift in the direction of individualism that focuses international attention on personal human rights rather than only on the rights and privileges of national sovereignty.

When humanitarian aid is almost the only international response to a crisis, and when that aid makes no distinction between different categories of victim, then all catastrophes are reduced to their lowest common denominator—simple compassion on the part of the onlooker. In the process, humanitarian action can mask blame and obscure the obligation to intervene in other ways.

One improvement might be to change the focus from neutrality to an alternative principle—impartiality. Whereas neutrality is concerned with the warring parties, impartiality emphasizes the victims as individuals. The rights of the victims and the moral imperative of justice would take precedence over the old excuses of neutrality or sovereignty. Another fact that is exerting a powerful influence on the emerging post-Cold War patterns of international relations is the swift and nearly complete dominance of the global economic system by an American-led, knowledge-based, free market capitalism. Like the emphasis on human rights, this has important implications for preventive diplomacy, which ultimately has to deal with root causes of human afflictions that are very often found in the grossly unequal distribution of economic benefits.

It is this lack of will in the face of extraordinary suffering and social chaos that is so appalling. While the wealthy nations of the world ride the crests of technological advancement and market expansion, the poorer countries are left behind in the troughs of lagging development so that the separation between the haves and have-nots becomes even more extreme. Just as we can see the deadly cycle of unsanitary conditions and contaminated water in diseases like cholera, so now we can also see the vicious circle of crushing poverty, inadequate education, and poor health that drive societies toward destruction and set off desperate migrations. This is a highly unstable condition with ominous implications for the entire international system.

After World War II, the United States launched the Marshall Plan that provided massive economic aid to prevent the collapse of a war-shattered Europe. Now the challenges to political and social stability are much larger in both scale and complexity, but the international community seems to be incapable of rising to its responsibilities. The United Nations is hardly able to support itself, much less lead the way to a new world order, and the world's economic leaders are too preoccupied with their own narrow interests to do anything about it.

Much of the burden of preventive action meanwhile falls on a vast array of nongovernmental organizations, or NGOs, that provide humanitarian assistance, sponsor public health programs, promote human rights, monitor abuses, and perform other services all across the international front of social need. Their work involves a great many issues related to the cause of preventive action. One of the more difficult is the extent to which humanitarian assistance may or may not be used to influence political outcomes in a violent dispute. As a matter of policy or practical necessity, NGOs have often found themselves delivering food through governments that were violating human rights, simply because these governments controlled the distribution system. As a result, opposition groups fighting for democracy and individual human rights have been effectively cut out of the aid loop. Other NGOs have fought to get aid through to opposition forces even when, sometimes, this has involved clandestine operations with guerrillas. "Sans frontières" organizations believe they have a dual role to play, to provide aid to victims in the field, but also to speak out as witnesses to intolerable events.

The number of NGOs has expanded dramatically in recent years, and they have performed spectacularly in many troubled areas, where major powers have been absent or ineffective. But they also have their weaknesses; some NGOs have their own partisan religious or political agendas. Rather than promoting peaceful settlements of conflict or working to prevent potential conflicts, such agendas can continue or even stimulate violence. Furthermore, NGOs tend to become increasingly dependent on government financing as they grow larger. This results in their not being able to go where the need for prevention is paramount.

Throughout *Preventive Diplomacy*, there is an emphasis on the importance of humanitarian issues in preventive diplomacy; that focus obviously reflects my own background and bias. The humanitarian emphasis also reflects my belief that people of all classes, in all societies, all over the world would better understand the efforts of politicians and diplomats, if they could relate them to their own lives. I suggest this can be done by utilizing well known methods of public health and the common metaphors of medicine. I also suggest that peacekeepers could better appreciate their own potential and limitations, by comparing their techniques and results with those that have proved satisfactory in the ancient field of disease prevention. Humanitarian concerns and crises are, increasingly, the bases for international interventions. Epidemics, starvation, genocide, and gross violations of human rights are no longer considered as merely the internal problems of sovereign nations.

As dead victims floated over the waterfalls and clogged Lake Kivu, as rescuers discovered churches packed with the hacked bodies of those who had unwisely sought refuge in a house of God, as a million desperate people fled across the border to overwhelm the town of Goma, those who believed in preventive diplomacy had to face the depth of its failure in Rwanda. Warning signals of impending genocide were not heeded. The opportunity for timely intervention was shamefully missed. Early neglect allowed, like an infection gone wild, an outbreak of ethnic madness to spread through green hills and small villages, until almost a million men, women, and children were killed with clubs and machetes. And then, as so often happens in epidemics, the victors became the victims, and hundreds of thousands more perished in overcrowded and unsanitary camps where the evil seeds of hatred and ignorance allowed the festering sores of conflict to flourish.

Similar tragedies unfolded in Kosovo and Albania as the century stumbled to a bloody close. NATO, the most powerful military alliance in the world, bombed a state into submission but seemed surprised to realize that people flee bombs and war zones. Since adequate preventive plans did not exist, a million cruelly displaced persons ended up in poorly prepared refugee camps. To care for this vast number, awash in a chaotic world of conflicts, the NATO forces belatedly turned to the United Nations.

Wars, like epidemic diseases, usually sputter to an end, and exhausted populations then try to rebuild broken societies. However, enormous numbers of lives are lost in the process, and generations suffer when basic traditions and customs, as well as the infrastructure of schools, hospitals, and homes are destroyed. Hatreds flourish in refugee camps, and the seeds of new conflict take hold in fertile soil. One must break the cycle, try to prevent the recurrent tragedy and to stop wars before they start.

It is possible, with effort and training and cooperation, to cultivate a new culture, one where prevention is considered and funded as much as reaction. This is not an impossible dream. I submit this work with the hope that a new generation will force the current political system to devote the necessary energy and funds to prevent deadly conflicts before they scar the next century.

I've always been fascinated by foreign lands and different cultures. When I first spent a month in Calcutta in 1959, cows and insects hadn't entered my concept of an afterlife. In southern Sudan, the Dinka animist beliefs seemed to me as profound, and logical, as those of more established religions. In planning a volume on Traditions and Values, therefore, I gave equal weight to these customs and practices. Between my wife and me stands a dear Sudanese friend and coauthor of a number of my research papers, the distinguished Professor of Medicine at the University of Khartoum, Abdel Razak Mubarak. In the background is a seven foot tall Dinka. Missing from the photo, but not from the memory of this journey outside Malakal,

600 miles south of Khartoum, are the faces of two drunken soldiers who stopped our truck later that day. We were many miles from the nearest village, and it surely wouldn't have mattered to the soldiers if they shot and robbed us, their obvious intention. We managed to slip away—neither the first nor the last time that a bend in an African road brought the immediate, unexpected, but very real, threat of death; or of providential escape.

Traditions, Values, and Humanitarian Action
2003

Our most profound thoughts evolve, often very slowly, and coalesce, sometimes, into workable concepts only after prolonged gestation. Someone asked me at the conference that led to *Traditions, Values, and Humanitarian Action,* "How long did it take you to plan and organize this?" I thought for a moment and answered, "About forty years."

In the early 1960s, I worked for many months as a physician in southern Sudan. It was a time of great social unrest and revolution in an area long isolated from the impact of modernity. The missionaries, who provided the only health and educational services available, were ejected shortly after my arrival. I found myself the only doctor within hundreds of miles of roadless, swampy land, in the Nilotic Sudd, home of the Dinka, Nuer, and Shilluk tribes.

Offering basic emergency medical services exposed me to customs and practices of which, at that time, I was utterly ignorant. They were not based on our western traditions and values and, initially, seemed to me the relics of a primitive culture. Over months, however, I came to respect the strength and beauty of their ways and beliefs. I gradually learned to see long-horned cattle not merely as a symbol of wealth, but as a measure of a man's pride; I saw polygamy and family love in a new light. I worked with an indigenous "healer" as my therapeutic partner. Together we saved some lives and helped alleviate much suffering, but part of the "therapy" was chicken bones and burnt cow dung, and I quickly and humbly came to understand that the local population, my patients, believed more in those modalities than in the incomprehensible antibiotic pills I provided.

Shortly thereafter, I began a series of studies in Somalia and spent part of every year for the next thirty-five years traveling with nomads across the Horn of Africa. The Somalis had no written language at that time, and I spent many nights, under brilliant stars and the Southern Cross, around campfires listening to their songs and *gabays,* the poetry of a proud people, in which they recorded, for future generations, how they survived epidemics and famines, and they told in rhyme of drought and warfare, and also, despite the incredible harsh landscape, of love and flowers, of the joy of rain and of camels giving birth. This immersion in Somali culture utterly changed my perceptions of human dignity and strength. I learned how traditions and values allowed clans to handle severe deprivations without complaint. The Somalis faced death with courage, with loyalty, and with protection and care for their most vulnerable. Even in the midst of conflict, or in the face of starvation, I was always safe, for I was their guest.

I was in Somalia when the nation was born, and I was there when it collapsed in the early 1990s. The soul of the people had been destroyed by corruption, oppression, the introduction of alien, selfish ways and the gradual abandonment of their own ancient ethos. Sadly, but inexorably, traditional customs that had bound the people together were shattered. There was no longer respect for the aged, for women, for religious leaders. The gun ruled the countryside. The fault lines got ever wider and Somali society, and the new nation, came crashing down.

Even earlier, in the late 1950s, I had worked in Calcutta, and there I learned that cows could be sacred and insects so precious that one wore face masks to prevent accidentally inhaling them. I spent my mornings at the School of Tropical Medicine, and for the rest of the hot, sweaty day I worked with Mother Theresa and her dying brood. She did not question the beliefs of those she cared for—they were human beings and that was enough. That was my introductory lesson on how the traditions and values of a people can influence the very process of death. Vast numbers of poor people were dying, and palliative care, any care, seemed to be a much appreciated gift from God. Providing medical care became a far more complex undertaking when one tried to serve a living population and a vibrant community in foreign lands.

For decades, I have been privileged to work in remote areas among people far removed from the effects—good and bad—of modernity. The more I traveled, and read, and participated in the daily lives of isolated tribes the more convinced I was that the richness of humanity lay in its incredible diversity. I do not share the belief that there is only one right way—whether that is how to rule, or how to worship, or court a mate, or establish a family, or express love, or even how to die. Any diminution in that diversity diminishes all of us. Attempts to homogenize the world, to impose uniform standards of behavior, to stifle differences of opinion and style, to impose restrictions on customs and practices because they are different from our own are regressive, usually destructive, acts. The biologic world thrives in its complexity, and artistic creativity flourishes best when there are multiple varying stimuli.

It was in this search for, and growing admiration of, other cultures that I watched, everywhere, people prefer to help more than harm their fellow man. What are the universal bases of these different traditions and value systems and how do they affect humanitarian action? What are the foundations on which we build caring societies? What are the acts we do—as individuals or as states—that can crack those foundations? And can anything be then done to put our humpty-dumpty world together again? *Traditions, Values, and Humanitarian Action* reflects that triad of questions.

Life is never secure, and the strongest foundations, so carefully constructed, can break under the pressure of fear, or folly, or evil. Fault lines in quake-prone areas cover moving earth plates that can collide and cause great damage. Individual—or governmental—acts that are in opposition to the foundations of a society can also cause devastation and destruction. This process can begin subtly. For example, it is almost easy to justify harsh interrogation methods of a suspected terrorist, but such an approach can lead, inexorably, to accepting dehumanizing torture as a legitimate tool of government. The world is now engaged in a "war on terrorism," a war without borders and, possibly, without end. Here the fault lines are potentially catastrophic. For example, especially in times of crises, one can be tempted to abandon, for short-term advantage, those precious civil liberties for—and on—which our nation was founded. Even easier, one can forsake international conventions that bind civilized states together even in times of war.

As we probe ever deeper, we attempt to elucidate those basic forces that both help and destroy mankind's noblest urges. *Traditions, Values, and Humanitarian Action* will, hopefully, stimulate the reader to appreciate the diverse strands that bind us together as a human family; to recognize those brutal acts that diminish the dignity of all mankind and endanger world stability and civilized intercourse; and, finally, in helping in the search for ways out of the current morass, it might encourage the reader to join the many thoughtful and good men and women who use their lives to foster the endless quest for peace, justice, and health around the world.

Technology for Humanitarian Action
2005

Hospitals, once charnel houses where the incurable and the contagious were isolated from contact with healthy society, and which then became holding pens to await the inevitability of death, are now centers of research and hope as well as service.

Physicians spend their days surrounded by the suffering of patients. To a degree, depending on the qualities of the varying doctors, the physician actually attempts to experience and share in that suffering so that comprehension of pain becomes an integral part of the healing process. Good physicians realize the privilege of their position – to be healthy and fit among the sick and maimed, to possess the powers and medicaments to relieve pain, to offer a cure to the despairing, and the glimmer of being able to "go on" to those who have lost all hope.

To fill his role successfully the physician must acquire the skill of detachment so that he can direct order out of chaos, arrest and change a fatal course of events. But that detachment need not be cold and selfish; in fact, it must be compassionate and involved so that a proper therapy can be fashioned for the particular needs of the individual patient. Wise physicians also know that every decision can make matters worse. If they make the wrong choice of a drug, or the timing of surgery and therapy, the patient may die an iatrogenic death. Even while providing correct therapy, doctors can cause extreme and unnecessary pain and suffering; consider the impact of aggressive chemotherapy or radical surgery removing vital organs to preserve the vestiges of life.

Now take the leap – and it is a quantum expansion of pain and suffering–to the situation that faces humanitarian workers following natural disasters and armed conflicts. Enter, in your minds, refugee camps where tens, and often hundreds of thousands of the innocent – mostly women, children, and the frail elderly – try to survive, unwanted and confused, hungry and ill in a devastated land, fearful for their lives and families, vulnerable to the prey of the conqueror or the lawless rabble. Think of the millions of internally displaced persons around the globe, not transient images on a TV screen, but real human beings fleeing from oppression and rape and starvation.

This situation is the modern, civilized hospital setting turned on its head; the luxury of individual care, the time for reflection, the cultivated niceties of medical service must be sacrificed in the early phases of a complex humanitarian emergency to the overwhelming need to impose an order and a system which can help save the greatest number of lives.

Here is where technology can complement compassion, can make possible the aspirations of the good physician or the skilled humanitarian worker. Without drawing on the technical capabilities – and potential – of the most advanced nations, those caught up in the almost endless maelstrom of humanitarian crises that scar our earth will continue to needlessly suffer and die.

Technology for Humanitarian Action offers seeds of hope for a world in desperate need of fresh ideas and solutions. It brings together, within the covers of a book, some of the finest minds in the field of technology and links their efforts, previously largely devoted to critical defense issues, to the problems faced daily by humanitarian workers. Our hope is also that those who read this volume will find their own innovative ways to share in, and help alleviate, the sufferings of mankind.

The Pulse of Humanitarian Assistance
2007

Everything evolves and grows or it stagnates and dies. This is clearly true in nature, where plants and animals need to constantly adapt for their species to survive. It is also obvious that the philosophic, economic and even religious bases of civilization change in response to unforeseen challenges, sometimes influenced by new technology and knowledge, often in reaction to failures.

In this sad, almost patently self-destructive era, those of us privileged to work in humanitarian assistance find ourselves struggling to maintain noble traditions. At times it seems we are trying to help the victims of natural disasters or armed conflicts with tools and approaches that may have been better suited to the political structures of earlier generations.

Compassion, sensitivity, respect for the dignity of every person, and, ultimately, love are but some of the timeless virtues that motivate our actions. Yet still more is needed. Competent, professional and effective programs in complex emergencies demand new techniques and improved skills. Over the centuries the rules, regulations and usual practices of humanitarian assistance have evolved. We must recognize that change is neither inherently good nor bad. But adhering rigidly to the standard approaches of the past is an almost certain recipe for failure. We should be able to adapt without abandoning fundamental values.

Taking the pulse—a basic diagnostic tool in medicine—is an ancient and trusted clinical exercise. At the bedside the physician uses a gentle, tactile measurement to see if the patient has a strong and steady circulation or one that is weak, irregular, thready, or even terminal. Taking the pulse is often the initial test performed by a medical doctor trying to establish an objective record rather than depending merely on a patient's subjective complaints. The nature of the pulse may lead to more refined studies, gradually building a foundation for rational therapy. Trying to detect a pulse is often the final act for a physician trying to determine if life has passed into death.

The Pulse of Humanitarian Assistance considers the pulse of humanitarian action today. It attempts to diagnose some of the major current problems that afflict the humanitarian profession; it also offers prognoses—predicting a way forward. If one is to address human suffering in the chaos that characterizes complex humanitarian crises, especially those in the developing world, then the etiologic significance of poverty and ignorance, corruption and incompetence, and the all too often evil effects of religion and politics are areas of study as valid as the life cycles of microbes. Professionals in humanitarian assistance must try to measure these factors constantly, just as one carefully records the pulse on the bedside chart of a sick patient.

For example, the semantic specificity that is expected in medicine is equally necessary in disaster management. "Humanitarian crises" are rarely the result of just a failure of the humanitarian system. Solutions, therefore, will not be found by merely addressing unmet humanitarian needs. It is often a dangerous and deceptive exercise to indulge in a "humanitarian intervention," implying that supplying food, water, shelter or medical relief satisfies obligations when, in reality, such activities are often only a convenient way for governments to avoid dealing with difficult underlying political or military problems. The awareness that humanitarian aid can be a "band-aid" approach – satisfying but ultimately futile – is a humbling but essential realization for those who accept leadership positions in the field.

Even in Chaos
2010

The prioritizing of health care in or just after wide-scale emergencies is done by a process called triage. The goal is to identify and assist the viable and devote available resources and manpower to assure that as many as possible of those injured survive. In the medical sphere – and I now this best as a physician who has worked extensively in conflict, post-conflict and disaster situations – trained personnel must make rapid decisions as to who can be helped, and in what order. Medical triage is based on clinical judgment, rules and standards derived from the difficult experiences of previous disasters. The early phase of such triage operations are dramatic – the stuff of television shows and movies – and often profoundly unsatisfying. One prays for the calm, the time when a multipronged therapeutic approach can be possible.

That is when all the many contributors needed to address complex humanitarian crises begin to serve as full and equal partners. Post-conflict operations demand many skills and are successful only when there is full coordination. Every profession is tempted to deceive itself that in resolving crises their contribution is the most important. Medical personnel, maybe more than most, may erroneously view the healing arts as the *sine qua non* in collaborative efforts.

Unfortunately, education has often been considered an indulgence that can be postponed till the development phase of reconstruction. That approach not only fails to provide an essential and comprehensive right of education for all, but it also denies to innocent, vulnerable children in need the critical protection that schools, educational safe places, provide. Education in such settings can also impart live-saving knowledge required by parents and youngsters learning how to survive in new and dangerous environments.

To again use the medical model, once the immediate hemorrhage has been stanched, and basic supports implemented to sustain life, the good physician has the rehabilitation specialist and psychiatrist, among others, begin to address the inevitable complications of severe trauma. So too at the communal level, humanitarian workers caring for those caught in the confusion and turmoil of life that is reality after conflicts and disasters, must simultaneously initiate multiple programs to promote a rapid return to normality, and to protect the young from further predictable assaults.

Education is now recognized as an essential ingredient in every conflict and disaster response. Here schools—and using the broadest concept of education—are critical. For children, education represents the only proven path to growth, development and peace.

My own awareness of the significance of education in conflict, post-conflict and disaster situations was part of the humbling process of being a Western-trained physician evolving into a humanitarian worker. I had been taught how to diagnose and treat patients. But specializing in tropical medicine brought early experiences in large epidemics and an appreciation of the plight of large dispossessed and vulnerable populations. Suddenly one had to learn how to deal with hundreds, thousands and tens of thousands of women and children in dire straits, to be adaptable and to function within very different cultures.

One quickly realized that individual diagnosis and therapy was a luxury one simply could not afford. One learned to coordinate food, water and sanitation programs, recognizing the public health imperatives of these nonclinical disciplines. In every refugee setting that I have known, the first sign of stabilization is the almost universal desire of mothers and children to establish a secure space for play and learning – the seeds of an educational operation.

Establishing islands of tranquility that schools – even the most basic safe space devoted to the young – creates one of the most wondrous and satisfying sights in any refugee camp. To see children recapture innocence, learn together and to hear them laugh again, and play, is one of the great rewards of hard, lonely humanitarian work. Schools provide the setting where feeding programs save lives; it is also where children are first made aware of the dangers of war zones – how to avoid unexploded land mines and evil adults who may seek to abuse or conscript the young as soldiers, sex slaves or hostages for ransom.

Education is a manifestation of society's belief that somehow, someday, somewhere there will be a life after the near death that children experience in conflict and post-conflict situations. *Even in Chaos* reflects the growing global commitment of the United Nations, its Member States, international and local non-governmental organizations, and concerned individuals that all children, everywhere, even under the most horrific conditions, have a right to education.

More With Less
2012

Humanitarian workers, if they are to be effective, must be realists. They deal every day with the cruel facts of human suffering, and no amount of rhetoric can alleviate pain or provide sustenance in times of widespread natural or human-made crises. *More With Less* reflects the reality that resources available for disaster preparedness and disaster response have been seriously diminished by the current global economic recession. It documents the evolution of global philanthropy, while also examining alternative methods to reduce costs through better preventive programs and suggesting potential sources for additional future funding for relief operations. It is not unrealistic for international humanitarian workers to believe that we can do more with less.

Humanitarian assistance is a discipline that attracts men and women who, in often terrible situations, continue to strive for a better world. They have dreams and visions, values and traditions that have not been suppressed by many earlier challenges. In fact, improvements in disaster prevention and response have often come because of adversity. These improvements – the establishment of accepted standards for health, shelter, food, protection, human rights, education; a code of ethics for workers; an emerging body of human rights and humanitarian law – have all been realized by learning lessons from past, often flawed, humanitarian missions. They have also, very significantly, been accomplished without abandoning the noble principles of independence, neutrality, and impartiality that are the foundation for our work.

One of the main dangers ahead, it seems to me, is that this very foundation may be destroyed in the name of bureaucratic efficiency and fiscal concerns. If the special role of international humanitarian work is not recognized then it will quickly be subordinated to military and political forces, especially in complex humanitarian crises and conflict situations.

When the UN Charter was drafted in 1945, there was but a single mention of humanitarian affairs. Maybe understandably, in the terrible afterglow of World War II, the Charter focused on human rights and the prevention of conflict. The Charter has, as its foundation, the sovereignty of Member States. International humanitarian action often necessitates cross-border activities in order to offer relief for victims. For that reason, humanitarians also contend that their work warrants respect for a neutral – as opposed to political – space in which they can provide impartial assistance to all in need.

There seems to be an inherent conflict in these views on sovereignty (at least as understood at the birth of the UN) and on intervention (as based on evolving concepts of the obligations of a State toward its citizens). Suffice it to note here that the full history of the UN is, fortunately, far more nuanced than the words of the Charter.

While the Charter is almost silent on humanitarian assistance, the deeds of the organization speak for themselves. UN-led relief operations actually predate the final signing of the Charter. The United Nations Relief and Rehabilitation Agency (UNRRA) was its first major international operation, offering critical help across the destroyed landscape of Europe, addressing hunger and other needs of refugees as World War II was winding down. When the United Nations Children's Fund (UNICEF) was founded in 1946, the "E" stood for Emergency, signifying its orientation to assist children anywhere, even across conflicted borders.

Later, in 1949, the United Nations Relief and Works Agency (UNRWA) was created to serve some 780,000 Palestine refugees who had been displaced in camps across a half-dozen countries. The United Nations High Commissioner for Refugees (UNHCR) was established in 1950 to deal with refugees fleeing as the Iron Curtain descended over Eastern Europe.

As the Cold War ended, and international attention could be focused on the former proxy states of the Big Powers, the UN gradually assumed an even greater role in humanitarian work. UNHCR became a major provider in the Balkan conflicts of the early 1990s. A UN role as coordinator of relief efforts had been formalized by the establishment of a separate United Nations Department for Relief Operations (UNDRO) in 1972. But that mandate was only limited to natural disasters. It was after the Cold War that the United Nations Department of Humanitarian Affairs (DHA) was established in 1991 to address all disasters, all around the world, and regardless of their cause. DHA was succeeded by the Office for the Coordination of Humanitarian Affairs (OCHA) in 1995.

These developments reflected the ability of the international community to better respond to complex humanitarian crises in zones formally under the absolute control of Big Powers. This period of a gradual evolution in our understanding of the nature of sovereignty, and of the tensions that exist between those who favor intervention over the absolute rights of states, is ongoing. The Responsibility to Protect (R2P) thesis has been used to justify various humanitarian interventions, but not without a growing concern about the limits and justification for such actions.

A further development at the UN–that the organization should deliver assistance "as one"–has inevitably increased the involvement of political and military actors in what had previously been solely the humanitarian domain based on principles of independence, neutrality, and impartiality. There are obvious dangers in "coordinating" responses by placing all efforts under one command. Military and political solutions to resolving complex humanitarian crises are the complete inverse of the traditional humanitarian approach. By definition, military and political positions are not neutral or impartial or independent.

The larger, more powerful actors are likely to dominate a response and implement "national interests," particularly those of the major powers. When former U.S. Secretary of State Colin Powell said he viewed humanitarian organizations as "force multipliers" for American policies in Iraq, there was widespread alarm in, and rejection by, international humanitarian nongovernmental organizations (NGOs). Nevertheless, pressures for such an approach, resulting in the destruction of humanitarian work as we have known it, are increasing.

The goal of complete coordination of UN activity in complex humanitarian crises may well destroy the very freedom that has made international humanitarian assistance so unique and effective for centuries. There is almost certain to be significant resistance to this approach. These challenges are complicated by the eroding financial base of traditional support for international disaster relief appeals. The current global economic crisis has put significant strain on many Western nations that have provided the majority of funds for past crises.

Books by Kevin M. Cahill, M.D. cited in this section

Health on the Horn of Africa
London: Spottiswoode Ballantyne, London, 1969.

The Untapped Resource: Medicine & Diplomacy
Baltimore: Orbis Press, Baltimore, 1973.

Irish Essays
New York: John Jay Press, New York, 1980.

Threads for a Tapestry
New York: New York Medical Press, New York, 1981.

Famine
New York: Orbis Press, New York, 1982.

The AIDS Epidemic
New York: St. Martin's Press, New York, 1983. Translated into Spanish, Portuguese, Japanese, French.

A Bridge to Peace
New York: 101 pp. Haymarket-Doyma, New York, 1988. Translated into Spanish, French, Italian, Arabic.

Imminent Peril: Public Health in a Declining Economy
New York: Twentieth Century Fund Press, New York, 1991.

A Framework for Survival: Health, Human Rights and Humanitarian Assistance in Conflicts and Disaster
New York: Basic Books/Council on Foreign Relations Publication, New York 1993. Revised Edition, New York: Routledge, New York, 1999.

Clearing the Fields: Solutions to the Global Landmine Crisis
New York: Basic Books/Council on Foreign Relations Publication, New York, 1994.

Preventive Diplomacy: Stopping Wars Before They Start
New York, Basic Books, New York, 1996. Revised Edition, Routledge, 2000. French Edition, Paris: Robert Laffont, Paris, 2005.

Traditions, Values and Humanitarian Action
New York: Fordham University Press, New York, 2003. French Edition, Paris: Robert Laffont, Paris 2005.

Technology for Humanitarian Action
New York: Fordham University Press, New York, 2005.

The Pulse of Humanitarian Assistance
New York: Fordham University Press, New York, 2007.

Even in Chaos: Education in Times of Emergency
New York: Fordham University Press, New York, 2010.

More With Less: Disasters in an Era of Diminishing Resources
New York: Fordham University Press, New York, 2012.

Forty-seven years after I first worked in Mogadishu, Somalia as a young physician leading a U.S. Navy medical research team I returned in late 2011 as the Chief-Advisor on Humanitarian and Public Health Issues for Nassir Abdulaziz Al-Nasser, the President of the United Nations General Assembly. Here we are exiting from a plane that had to use "evasive flying tactics" to *avoid missile fire as we landed. We donned helmets and flak jackets to tour the bombed out shell of Mogadishu, a city I knew well over many decades. It was a dangerous trip, and just days after our departure two of the very small NGO community with whom I met – physicians with Médicins Sans Frontières – were shot to death in their office. Why them – and not me – remains a*

*puzzle, as it has in similar circumstances in
all my life.*

Part Four: Personal

In the Introduction to this book I cited the profound influence my wife had—and still has—on every aspect of my life. When we were very young she would ask,"What makes you tick?" In this final section, I offer some articles and addresses that discuss my family, love, education, spirituality and suggest the seeds that she nourished so carefully for so many years.

The concluding article in this section brings us back to the opening essay, a report of a Pontifical Mission to war-torn Lebanon undertaken at the request of Pope John Paul II. After his death, at the request of Vatican colleagues, I wrote a brief reflection on the unusual privileges and potential that can emerge in the good physician-patient relationship.

Finally, I end this book with a poem Kate wrote for my 65th birthday, one that offers her definition of "what made—and makes—me tick."

God and My Life
2005

I have been asked, as part of the Lenten Series in this beautiful Church of St. Vincent Ferrer, to consider "The Role of God in My Life." This requires definitions – of "God" and "my life." Since I am not a theologian, and wisely avoid arcane arguments about the Almighty, I will approach the task with an emphasis on something about which I do know – "my life." I will try to use that exploration to then develop a concept of "God" that has its origins in a first-generation Irish household in the Bronx.

The immigrant relatives I can recall had a deep faith in the Roman Catholic Church, and much of the cycle of our lives was defined by weekly Confessions, Lenten fasts, First Friday Masses, Baptisms, Confirmations, and the celebrations of the joy of life at the birth of the baby Jesus at Christmas or the Resurrection from the dead on Easter morning. Nevertheless, we were taught not to be afraid, at least in the privacy of the home, to question both the pronouncements of religious leaders, or the logic of clerics, especially the official hierarchy.

There was a fundamental respect and loyalty to the Church but, again, this was tempered by a deep suspicion of pomposity and assumptions of unquestioned authority. We were told to beware of those "who genuflect too much", who deferred too easily to "the cloth," when they should be seeking justice and equity and truth, whatever that was. Also, as was typically Irish, dinner conversations were filled with probing questions regarding the mysteries of life.

My father was the first physician in a generation of police officers, and seemed to have inherited the mantle of family chieftain – at least for that part of the clan that multiplied in cold water flats from Fordham Road to Hell's Kitchen, and later out to Breezy Point and Belle Harbor. He had been well trained in Jesuit logic – some people claim that is an oxymoron – and he encouraged his children to parse and analyze diverse intellectual positions. At the end of the day he would probably accept an ex cathedra declaration by the Pope, but he sure didn't like it. He didn't want to miss the chance to argue every facet, to see and appreciate every side of every issue.

I can recall him, many times, at our dining room table

dissecting some finely nuanced theological positions with the local priest. It was an unfair intellectual battle, for the priest, who undoubtedly possessed profound faith had, nonetheless, little capacity to explain the basis for his devout beliefs, and my father would pursue the poor man till he surrendered with a defensive mutter: "Ah, but it's God's will." My father was a wise physician, and he knew life was rarely that simple. He would be the devil's advocate, one night defending monotheism, and the next arguing passionately for the rights of atheists or agnostics. We were expected to stand our ground, and defend our assigned positions.

Looking back on those wonder-filled years I am reminded of the dilemma faced by the Irish sisters in Brian Friel's play, *Dancing at Lunghasa*, when their beloved brother, a missionary priest in Africa having gone "slightly native," comes home and tries to explain the universality of religious beliefs, and the indigenous celebrations he would lead for his parishioners in appeasing a reluctant "rain God." The traditional Irish villagers didn't want to hear this heresy – they had their faith and their "God" – a complex Father, Son, and Holy Ghost arrangement – and that should be enough for anyone, especially a priest.

But is it? My early kitchen table education was broad and good enough to incorporate other views and, as I began my own life's journeys, I was very grateful for the stimulating, sometimes perverse, and peculiar philosophical foundation of youth. When I first went to India – more than 50 years ago – I worked in Calcutta, where the Hindu majority believe cows are sacred, and even flies and mosquitoes might possess, in their tiny bodies, a previous being. By the time I left Calcutta, after 4 months, I really wasn't certain that I might not be a cow in the next life, and I wasn't really certain it mattered much.

Helping people mattered. Seeing the unique, the beautiful – call it a soul, spirit, the hand of "God" – but finding something special in every human being became the *raison d'etre* for my life. Obsession with theological conformity and liturgical niceties simply didn't seem very important, as you discovered "God" in the Somali bush, or in a totally Islamic culture.

We lived for several years in the Middle East. When our second son was born there, I became very friendly with a local Italian missionary who baptized him. Fr. Ruffino once told me that as a young priest, he would measure his success in his first Chinese mission by the number of baptisms he would perform in a year and he would proudly send an annual report back to the Vatican. After decades of this satisfying service to the Church he was sent to Egypt where proselytizing for a non-Islamic religion was strictly forbidden, and converting and baptizing were grounds for expulsion. He had to change his criteria; he would give witness by simply being there, but all his other ceremonial roles as a priest were over. There was but one God, and Mohammed was his Prophet. Gradually Fr. Ruffino came to accept that his Arab neighbors were his family, no better, no worse than those he once washed free of Original Sin in the sanctified waters of Christ.

So where does this leave me in my search for "God"? A poet – who happened to be a Jesuit priest – once wrote of the odd manifestations of the Almighty. Gerard Manley Hopkins discovered Christ, not in vestments, or on an altar, but in everyday life:

Glory be to God for dappled things –
For skies of couple-colour as a brinded cow;
For rose-moles all in stipple upon trout that swim;
Fresh–firecoal chestnut–falls; finches' wings;
Landscape plotted and pieced-fold, fallow,
And plough;
And all trades, their gear and tackle and trim.

All things counter, original, spare, strange;
Whatever is fickle, freckled (who knows how?)
With swift, slow; sweet, sour; adazzle, dim;
He fathers–forth whose beauty is past change:
              Praise him.

I think that is where I come out. After many years of medical practice, long periods of loneliness and reflection in what some would call the God-forsaken deserts of Somalia, or the swamps of Sudan, or working all over the world amidst refugees in the chaos that follows war and natural disasters, I found my own spiritual strength.

I can identify with the Christ who came down to wash feet,

know rejection and die on a cross. Hidden in the humble, sacred pockets of life are the good thieves who will go to paradise, the trusting leper who will be cured. The Resurrection, to me, is reflected everyday in the tenacity and nobility of sick people, and the remarkable resilience of men, women, and children, often against overwhelming odds.

The plight of the poor, the rights of the oppressed, the anguish and chaos of epidemics, and complex humanitarian crises have been my chosen fields. I think part of this identity, and solidarity with the outcasts of society, stems from my own Irish immigrant background and from the almost overwhelming significance of family and love in my life.

For many years I have devoted much of my non-clinical energies in trying to identify workable bridges between medicine, public health, and the softer discipline of diplomacy. One only has to work in conflict zones for a very short time to appreciate the dehumanizing effects of fear, injury, rape, or even of survival under appalling refugee conditions. No avenue can be left untried in the search to heal the wounds of war and build a new peace.

When combatants can agree on little else they sometimes – not always – will cease killing and maiming only for a humanitarian effort – one that can often help both sides. Using this respect for health projects, we established "corridors of tranquility," neutral areas in bitter civil wars. These pauses allowed for discussion and dialogue; no matter how brief, they can provide the foundation blocks for eventual reconciliation.

It is sometimes difficult to talk about "God" to those intent on destroying their enemies, and formal religions have had a pretty dismal record in the search for peace. An inordinate amount of people still die because of differences over what is considered "the true faith", surely an odd justification for the slaughter of neighboring innocent civilians. In the former Yugoslavia, both former Secretary of State Cyrus Vance and Lord David Owen tried for three years to find a compromise to end the killing. They told me, in deep frustration, that none of the religious leaders – Muslim, Orthodox, or Roman Catholic – ever found the courage to move beyond their parochial concerns.

At Fordham University's Institute of International Humanitarian Affairs, we have recently initiated a project that will try to identify universal values, the common spirituality that seems to exist in all cultures, even during wars. All over the world different civilizations have developed methods – sometimes positive, sometimes negative – to prevent the worst excesses of war. These strands of humanitarian decency must be emphasized, and woven, not only into Geneva Conventions and legal documents, but into some commonly-accepted fabric so that we can learn to survive together, not threatened by, but actually celebrating the diversity of, mankind.

It is in this search for universal values, a search that may allow peace to be reborn from the ashes of war, that today I most clearly see "God." It is into that troubled gray zone of conflicts and reconstruction that I hope "God" will help guide me in leading a better life of service to those in need.

The Influence of Yeats
Georgetown University, 1988

What they undertook to do
They brought to pass;
All things hang like a drop of dew
Upon a blade of grass.

W. B. Yeats,
"Gratitude to the Unknown Instructors"

As we gather to celebrate the bicentennial of this great university, its present leaders asked that I reflect on liberal education, human excellence, and classic texts, and on our own evolution as the products of an academic tradition trained to draw from, and maybe even add to, that special body of literature that shapes our youthful dreams, encourages mature aspirations, and replenishes, over and over again, the spirit that struggles for integrity, purpose, and sometimes survival in a system that too often seems to reward only mediocrity and conformity. Your president asked that I provide a focus to this exercise by selecting the single book, from a lifetime's readings, that I had consulted most often – a very interesting challenge. In fact, the text was not hard to find. A well-worn volume,

The Collected Poems of W. B. Yeats, it lay by my bedside, as it has since it was given to me (as the inscription by my father reminds me) when I was twelve. Since then, it's been alongside me wherever I've been—through college and medical school, through the pivotal period as a young Navy physician in Africa, through courtship and marriage and the birth of our sons, in good times and bad, through all the years that sometimes now can seem *From our birthday until we die / Is but the winking of an eye.*

I come before you as the product of a Jesuit education, but one that, as I shall try to explain, began in infancy and was influenced in childhood by the orations and idiosyncratic logic of my father who often transferred his Regis, Fordham, and Georgetown views of the world to his offspring through the medium of poetry. My own university years at Fordham added a bit of polish to that familial foundation.

Now most of the new knowledge that flows, or trickles, into the reservoir of my learning comes primarily from my sons who, happily, carry home (and onto their secular universities and lives) Regis and Loyola influences that, at least to their grateful parents, seem beneficially formative. Not everyone has viewed Jesuit education so positively, and it might be well, as we begin this bicentennial weekend, inundated, I will presume, with congratulatory notes—including a message from the President of the United States—to recall that two of his predecessors in the White House did not greet the restoration of the Jesuits in the land of the free with any enthusiasm.

In 1816, John Adams wrote to Thomas Jefferson: "I do not like the resurrection of the Jesuits... who are more numerous than everybody knows... in as many shapes and disguises as ever the King of Gypsies himself assumed: in the shape of Printers, Editors, Writers, School Masters, etc. If ever any Congregation of Men could merit eternal perdition on Earth and in Hell... it is the Company of Loyola." Had Adams employed a speechwriter, he no doubt would have dubbed the Jesuits "an evil empire."

But, somehow, the nation survived and thrived, along with Georgetown, the mother of a long line of Catholic colleges and universities that have played such a prominent role in the intellectual life of America. They have provided, as has the book I have chosen, a unique view on national debates, an historical and religious perspective that allows one to find joy in sorrow and avoid, sometimes, the temptations of the latest vogue. We convene at a time in history when fundamental questions are being posed regarding our role, not only as powerful leaders in an increasingly divided world but as fellow human beings that share a single planet and a finite time on earth.

The literary career of William Butler Yeats spanned more than a half-century. His *Collected Poems* offer, therefore, as do our lives and, hopefully, our education, a temporal, developmental aspect which a single text, technical or literary, cannot provide. The collection moves from the simple rhymes of childhood through the passionate poems of physical desire, from the attempts to capture myths and theological theories in iambic pentameter to single, memorable lines that distill the universal experiences of combat and confusion, rejection and despair, and lead, ultimately, to a wisdom that has been a source of strength and courage at different stages of my life.

I should, I believe, begin my reflections on *The Collected Poems* with two cautions. First, like the rest of us, Yeats was far from perfect, and – at times – as wrong headed as a person can be. One does not read poetry to support a thesis or buttress an argument as one might utilize journals in preparing a scientific paper. To draw solace and inspiration from his poems is not to embrace his entire philosophy. His ideas were not always admirable, and sometimes, they were so base as to be despicable. It would be difficult, for instance, even to attempt to defend Yeats's period of neo-Nazi Blue Shirt fascination, were it not that one can almost feel a poetic soul groping for order.

Second, I am not a Yeatsian academician in the sense that would be required were I seeking a faculty position in your English department. Scholars may analyze and annotate and even deconstruct Yeats's text, but I, fortunately, am in a position to use his volume only as a basis for the personal reflections asked by your president. Even if I had the knowledge – which I do not – to present myself as an authority, I would side with Yeats who wondered:

What would they say
Did their Catullus
Walk that way.

With those caveats in mind, let me try to share with you the pervasive influence of Yeats's poems on a single life. In doing so, I will relate what is, necessarily, a highly individual view of how and to what degree a liberal education fashioned my own concepts of, and aspirations towards, human excellence, how the Jesuit inspired teachings of both father and sons have opened the mind so that education leads not to a conclusion but to unimagined frontiers, so that the journey of discovery ends, hopefully, only with death and that the sense of mission we inherit—and transmit—is the great unfinished gift we celebrate in these ancient halls of learning.

Childhood

My exposure to Yeats's poems began in a Bronx Irish immigrant household where oral tradition held sway, and we truly felt sorry for those who were missing the excesses we thought were normal. Oh, we probably knew, even as children, that there was too much alcohol consumed and the roast beef shouldn't always be charred, but somehow the joy of having my father recite long poems made dinnertime magical.

My earliest recollection of a Yeats poem is, probably at age four or five, hearing the lilt of his lullaby:

The angels are stooping
Above your bed;
They weary of trooping
With the whimpering dead.

And now, a generation later, as my five sons leave the nest to fashion their independent lives, I often find myself thinking of the last lines of that poem,

I sigh that kiss you,
For I must own
That I shall miss you
When you have grown.

Yeats held his place in those Sunday night festivals of love somewhere between Robert Service and Catullus, a definite notch below *The Aeneid* and *The Odyssey*, which were recited, repetitively, in the Latin and Greek my father had learned from the Jesuits. The Cahills were, we were told, descendants of the High Kings of Ireland; even if the throne now apparently stood in Uncle Dinny's coldwater flat in the Bronx, there was still a genetic nobility we accepted and treasured. There was an emphasis on integrity and honesty, on love and loyalty, on the need to dream of things that never were, and the willingness to openly share these fantasies with family. If Hirsch's anthropologic theory of education (in *Cultural Literacy*) is valid, then it was those early ethnic experiences that were woven, strand by spoken strand, into patterns which preserved for a new generation both Cahill traditions and our distinctive means of communication.

The early years of childhood and adolescence were a privileged period of protected discovery. Particularly in a large, close family, before the identity of each emerges, one's self seemed but an extension of an already existing organism. We were happy and secure in a home life that I can recall as vividly as the poet remembers Innisfree:

And I shall have some peace there, for peace
comes dropping slow,
Dropping from the veils of the morning to where
the cricket sings;
There midnight's all a glimmer, and noon
a purple glow,
And evening full of linnet's wings.

Those were innocent days in a seaside town, and in the undeveloped parts of the Bronx where many roads where not yet paved, and patients paid my physician-father with eggs and goat's milk. It was a time—even as World War II began—of dreams:

I walk among long dappled grass
And pluck till time and times are done
The silver apples of the moon,
The golden apples of the sun.

Our childhood instruction was not devoid of content, and academic advancement was certainly carefully monitored; but as I look back now, the important lessons, the beginnings of a true liberal education, were begun in the home, not the school. There were goals and accomplishments that could not be measured with grades but were understood, even then, to be far more important than the formal academic curriculum. Somehow the liberal education that leads us into our own souls, that defines how we make judgments and girds us for the struggles that even a child sees coming was transmitted, at least in my instance, from father to son in lines of poetry.

We learned from ballads and myths that troubled seas were an inevitable part of the journey of life. The odes and stories – as well as the foibles of innumerable relatives – made us aware, in those gentle introductory courses to maturity, that not always would we *dance upon the shore* nor be bothered by *the wind or waters roar,* that sooner or later we would not merely *lie long and dream in the bed / of the matching of ribbons for bosom and head.* In every good tale there came a time when *the seed of the fire flickered and grew cold,* and we were taught not to fear the unknown.

Education, right from the start, should liberate not only the mind but the heart and even the soul. Stories should emphasize tolerance and expose the folly of prejudice; *For arrogance and hatred are the wares / Peddled in the thoroughfares.* To become free and independent it helps to have a foundation rooted in ancient myths, for even as one grows with age and experience, readings and travel, there is a baseline against which one compares new information and those first temptations of a wider world – *I knew a phoenix in my youth, so let them have their day.* Even if we suspected our ties to those ancestral Kings of Ireland were not quite legitimate, we learned to view, with regal disdain, titles and mere material goods, the artificial power of politicians and even "the cloth."

In a large family, immersed in Yeats, one learned to be tolerant, not *to quarrel with a thought because it was not their own,* and to avoid the tragic trap of calling *pleasures evil that happier days thought good.* Maybe one needs the innocence and security of youth to completely believe that:

For the good are always merry
Save by an evil chance,
And the merry love the fiddle,
And the merry love to dance.

But what a difference that view of the world makes as one prepares for sorrows and struggles, the reality of maturity. Most of all, in a childhood filled with Yeats and the residue of my father's Jesuit liberal education, we learned about love, learned through literature how to approach adolescence, how to reach out and appreciate what was rare and unique in other people, to treasure those *moments of glad grace,* the beauty of *a pilgrim soul* and *the sorrows of your changing face.* We were taught to *dream of soft looks and of shadows deep,* to learn about gentleness and reverence, to begin to relate, and even compete, without violence, to understand the value and the power of words as weapons for the inevitable battles to come:

They have spoken against you everywhere
But weigh this song with the great and their pride;
I made it out of a mouthful of air,
Their children's children shall say they have lied.

These were the lessons we took from youth, the lasting gifts of a home filled with love and passionate rhyme. Though they now are but *memories, vague memories,* they remain the core and compass of my life.

University Days
The search for self took Yeats, as it takes many of us, down paths that prove fruitless and, in retrospect, slightly embarrassing. There is dalliance with various intellectual and social fads, when every passing fancy tempts you from your chosen craft. There are obsessions with dress and style, maximalist and minimalist, reflecting both the exuberance and the tragedy that the young begin to sense in the world at large.

There are the temptations–based on false arrogance–to judge oneself superior to the hordes of plain, unlettered humanity who daily wrench an existence from life through sweat and toil and sacrifice. Yeats, the Anglo-Irish aristocrat, noted archly at this period in his own life that his blood had not passed through *any huckster's loins,* as did that of the cattle and horse selling, shopkeeping population he disdained in Ireland – and as did, I'll assume, the seed of most of my own immigrant forebears.

Like Yeats, most of us pass through similar phases, especially if we are blessed with the good fortune to attend a university where the privileged can convene and blossom in early adulthood. The elitism and mystery of fraternities and clubs, the initiation rights, the easy assumption of superiority are almost predictable aberrations. But the early principles and values ingrained at home and the influence of wise professors, make these aberrations difficult to sustain for too long. If we're lucky, we move on to the fuller, more fulfilling life the university offers.

This is the time when one attempts, as a twenty-three year old Yeats noted, *to hammer your thoughts into unity,* when *the fascination of what's difficult has dried the sap out of my veins,* when men wear themselves out with dreams and passions. Gradually, one takes all these experiences, lays the template of those precious lessons of childhood over them, and fashions tools for self-discovery, fulfillment, or survival. The rewards of a humanistic education are distilled into a way of life where innocence is not lost but rather refined, where curiosity replaces false confidence, and where humility and modesty are understood, and a gentle and generous understanding of others' faults and gifts evolve. One learns the importance of manners – *In courtesy I'd have her chiefly learned; / Hearts are not had as a gift but hearts are earned.* And one becomes aware of the rights and the rituals of courtship – *Ceremony's a name for the rich horn / And custom for the spreading laurel tree.* These are the years Georgetown celebrates, that critical stage when young men and women, for two hundred years, have come to you seeking definition, fashioning an ethos, learning to inherit, from learned guides, the best from the past and preparing to transform and transmit this experience to their own and to the next generation.

Hopefully they have learned how to handle rejection and despair as well as happiness and success. The harsh experiences of adult life are made tolerable by the lessons of the liberal education begun in childhood and polished in the classrooms of life.

It's the time of life when I began to glimpse the meaning and the wisdom – inaccessible to a child – of the lines Yeats wrote for one who had to deal with sordid and unfair causes for failure. The training of youth, the poet hoped, had bred his friend *to a better thing than triumph* and would allow him to *be secret and exult,* even in defeat. The armor of a liberal education begins to shine.

It's a time when we learn, in Yeats's words, *that all is changed, changed utterly / A terrible beauty is born.* The graduate must ultimately go forth from such hallowed protected halls as these, using all that has been stored in that *rag and bone shop of the heart,* all that has been absorbed from family and teachers. He or she may find their *embroidered coat* of worldly training torn by competitors, but now the wise owners will realize that such information is but a superficial covering on the secure base of a liberal education. In fact, there may be, as we almost always come to understand, times in life when there is as much *enterprise in walking naked.*

International Health and Foreign Policy

All these bits and pieces of our past eventually coalesce, if we are fortunate, and prepare us for the ultimate challenges, the roles we may be unexpectedly asked to play along life's erratic pilgrimage.

Cultural and ethnic pride, themes of emerging nationalism, and questions as to what constitutes patriotism permeate the poetic lines of middle-aged Yeats. He served as a senator of the Free State and spoke nobly, if unsuccessfully, in his government's debates on censorship, divorce, artistic freedom, and education. Those public years find themselves in his poems on *Church and State, On Being Asked for a War Poem,* and *Easter 1916.*

Gradually, with more experience and insight, he became disillusioned with the self-serving aspects that seem to characterize so much of what is euphemistically called "public service." He castigated the *Leaders of the Crowd*

They must to keep their certainty accuse
All that are different of base intent;
Pull down established honor; hawk for news
Whatever their loose fantasy invent.

And in *Nineteen Nineteen*, Yeats bitterly denounced the distortion that politicians can create even from the dreams of independence:

We who seven years ago
Talked of honor and truth,
Shriek with pleasure if we show
The weasel's twist, the weasel's tooth.

My own pilgrimage led from college to medical school and eventually in directions never imagined even among all the visions my father spun out of words at the dinner table in the Bronx. I am a physician who has had the good fortune to work in troubled areas of Africa, Latin America, and Asia for the past quarter century. I have seen war and revolution, earthquakes and droughts, famine and floods. I have established national health services in poverty stricken Third World countries that had few doctors, sometimes none. I also directed, for six years, the most complex state medical system in the United States. Yeats captured in a few lines why I entered, and continue to find great satisfaction in, public health among the poorest.

The wrong of unshapely things is a wrong too
great to be told;
I hunger to build them anew and sit on a green
knoll apart...

To respond to the initial question your president asked in inviting me to this convocation – Why do you do the things you do? – I shall try, with stories of two tropical areas, to link that liberal education I have described to the unusual challenges my professional career has offered. These experiences may strike a resonant note in your minds or – even better – a dissonant one that will lead to lively discussion. Along the way, it will be clear, I hope, how the poems of Yeats, constantly reread, have continued to offer guidance, frequently much more guidance than all the knowledge and training acquired in medical school.

The Sudan
I once ran a clinic in Fashoda, six hundred miles south of Khartoum, where Marchand and Kitchener held their

momentous meeting that carved up the colonial map, and the lives, of modern Africa. No one consulted the "natives"; they were naked and primitive and couldn't speak our language and didn't, until they were forced to, worship our God. But one only worked among the Shilluk and Nuer and Dinka for a short time before one realized they had retained their ancient crafts and understood the ways of the river and the beauty of the swamps better than the white man could imagine.

Because the missionaries were ejected from southern Sudan while I was there in the early 1960s, I found myself as the only physician within hundreds of miles in any direction. There were no courses in medical school that prepared one for these challenges, for understanding that pride and tradition and culture were as essential as aspirin or bandages in running a rural medical program.

One came quite quickly to realize that prejudice and economic exploitation are realities that must be faced – and openly attacked – if one is to fulfill the obligations of the physician. It is necessary to appreciate the cry of the oppressed and the burden of ignorance and fear and poverty if one is to practice medicine in a developing land, especially during periods of chaos and disaster. There had been no lectures in the medical school curriculum that would help me establish refugee camps or deal with a system where cultural influences made it difficult, if not impossible, for nurses to care for the opposite sex. Our training in diagnosis and therapy had prepared one for the well-stocked consulting room but not for the grand scale that I now faced.

I discovered that ignorance and politics, racism and religion, weather and witchcraft were integral parts of most of the medical problems I had to deal with, and solutions were discovered more frequently in those Jesuit lectures on Aristotelian logic and Thomistic reasoning, on an understanding and humility first fostered in courses in comparative religion and in the bitter lessons of history, even if one also knew that most of the history we had learned was biased to glorify Western achievements.

I had never considered how to construct a health service in the middle of a war and how to do it with few supplies and only semi-skilled "dressers." The "witch doctor" had a hold on the community, but his results left much to be desired. Does one fight such a system using the formidable forces of science and technology, or should one accommodate, abandoning that superior perch we have built from knowledge and training, in order to serve the suffering? I saw no alternative, and we joined forces. He helped get me people to train and spread the word that my modern methods complemented his insights and skills.

These were experiences that tested the very core of a young doctor's soul. I recall staying up the first few nights after the missionary families and their followers fled. They had staffed the local hospital and dispensed all the medical care offered in an area that could cover the whole northeastern United States. I would deliver babies and sew up animal bites, try to dress fetid wounds, and even amputate gangrenous limbs. But finally, exhausted, I said I was going to sleep, and I did. They called me shortly thereafter to say a woman was bleeding, and I got up to help and then again went back to bed. And again they called, and I refused to get up. I said I couldn't survive if I didn't sleep and sent them away, and I slept soundly for ten hours. I don't know to this day what ingredients—apart from sheer exhaustion—led to that decision. But looking back, I'm sure that somewhere amidst all the nuances the Jesuits had taught me about facing such ethical and moral dilemmas, the lines of Yeats were mixed in: *Too long a sacrifice / Can make a stone of the heart.*

At any rate, I began a daily routine of hard work, during the day organizing a basic health service, sharing the satisfying credit with my "witch-doctor" friend, training volunteers in first aid, and going to sleep at night after a decent dinner of gazelle or quail. I stayed for months in southern Sudan and almost felt guilty realizing how much I enjoyed the bizarre experience. None of the doctors who replaced me stayed very long because they did not believe it was moral to leave the dying and go to bed. They felt that violated their Hippocratic oath and they would work nobly till they fell, which they usually did in a matter of days.

The program collapsed, the modern medical men went back to their laboratories and clinics, and the indigenous people to their own means and methods of survival. That experience was over twenty-five years ago, and civil war in the southern Sudan today poses the same dilemma for a young physician who might find himself or herself there today. What to do, how, why? Interesting questions, I think, for a community like Georgetown to consider as it ponders the uses of a humanistic education.

It takes time—and intimate experience—with *things uncomely and broken, all things worn out and old* to balance the romance of youth, to change the passion of love into caring and compassion. It is certainly safer to reap the rewards and stay within the expected confines of a medical career, but that was not what fate offered nor, it seemed to me, what the lessons of a liberal education demanded. Yeats noted that the parched tree of freedom is not watered by *polite meaningless words* but by that *excess of love* we had inherited in an immigrant home and honed in a Jesuit university.

Nicaragua

Medicine has allowed me to function in that fascinating interface where death and life coexist. I have come to appreciate, if not always fully understand, the multiple forces that influence human—and medical—reactions. Ideally, compassion and generosity are not merely individual traits; somehow a great nation—and as Americans we were taught that our good fortune and hard work had offered that global destiny—should fuse those personal qualities into national policies. I had been taught that my role as a citizen was to participate to the fullest extent possible in translating the dreams of our Founding Fathers into programs that would serve those less fortunate. That was also the essence of our theology courses, and philosophy professors promoted the necessary freedom of thought so we could—and would—pursue excellence wherever that search led.

At certain times in history, one must move beyond theory and dialectics. Mere acquiescence with the status quo can be as great a sin as an evil act of commission. Our liberal education not only gives us the capacity, but the obligation, to speak out against wrongs and argue for the oppressed. One can visit any hospital in Nicaragua today and see the effects of current policies perpetuated in the name of the American people. Mercenaries, completely funded by the United States, mine harbors, rape and kill to "protect" democracy. To protect our great land from the threat of an impoverished nation, we have instituted economic embargoes that prevent the most basic health care from reaching malnourished Nicaraguan civilians. There is nothing subtle about seeing a surgical operation done without anesthesia or watching a woman or baby strangle to death because spare parts for American built respirators and incubators can no longer be purchased.

Are we to be merely bemused when the name of the land we love is soiled by those whose major obsession, anticommunism, is used to justify any sordid means? How does one deal with those who find it easier to violate than to heal, who employ deceit and semantic fantasies to cover their folly?

As Yeats asked:

For how can one compete,
Being honor bred, with one
Who, were it proved he lies,
Were neither shamed in his own
Nor in his neighbors' eyes?

One does not have the privilege of silence if one seeks the answer in a Managua hospital.

Unfortunately, our TV leaders, the blow-dried politicians on one-day tropical tours never smell the gangrenous limbs or feel the feverish head of a dying child. Their airport interviews and pompous pronouncements are devoid of the humility – and shame – that come from firsthand experience in any Nicaraguan clinic or ward. Yeats understood the tragedy that ideologues impose, the chaos that flows from policies built on fear and hatred, on continuing economic exploitation, and on the arrogant assumption that any nation – ours included – has a monopoly on wisdom or a divine right to dictate to others trying to regain their almost forgotten identity. He wrote how, *Things fall apart; the center will not hold / Mere anarchy is loosed upon the world* and he warned that, *The best lack all conviction while the worst / Are full of passionate intensity.*

I have tried to capture in recent books some of my anger at missed opportunities and have offered a direct response to those who confuse power with oppression. I fully realized my positions might well be unpopular with the privileged few who presume to shape our foreign policy. But it required little courage to identify with those who suffer and die in the man-made hell we have created in Nicaragua.

Conclusion
In honor of the two hundredth anniversary of a great university, and in response to the fascinating challenge to select a single text and reflect on the relationship between liberal education and human excellence, I have, with much pleasure, returned to the Yeats that thrilled me when first I heard it recited by my father, that inspired me when I was young, that helped me in courtship and in learning to love, that gave me the courage to make decisions in my professional career when there were few – or no – precedents on which to base actions. His words have also sustained me during those inevitable periods of rejection and apparent defeat.

At the end of his long poetic career, Yeats left one final gift, a revised order for his *Last Poems*. Rather than conclude with the cryptic lines carved on his tombstone: *Cast a cold eye / On life, on Death / Horseman pass by* he chose, as his ultimate statement, the poem, *Politics*. In it, Yeats captures, in memorable couplets, themes that have profoundly affected me and that I raised for your consideration today. With the wisdom of age, the poet suggested a perspective that included a healthy skepticism of worldly titles and the trappings of power. He focused, rather, on the priority of memory and, most importantly, stressed the eternal, re-creating force of love in the wondrous cycle of life.

How can I, that girl standing there,
My attention fix
On Roman or on Russian
Or on Spanish politics?
Yet here's a traveled man that knows
What he talks about,
And there's a politician
That has read and thought,
And maybe what they say is true
Of war and war's alarms,
But O that I were young again
And held her in my arms.

I am grateful to the Georgetown family for inviting me to join in your celebration, and thank all of you for being here and sharing in this journey of discovery.

The boys of summer, with their 5'6" Chief
Lifeguard. Establishing the criteria by
which one judges the outside world, as
well as one's self, is part of the process of
maturation. It is very important to learn,
early in life, that mere physical attributes
must be balanced with intellectual and
creative assets that, in the long, and even
in the short, run are far more important.

Yeats wished his daughter not "beauty
overmuch," worrying that she might come
to believe that what she saw in the
"looking glass" would substitute for those
qualities that ultimately win respect
and lasting love.

Even knowing all that, however, and
philosophically sound as that awareness
may be, those sunny days were an

enormously satisfying, and happily remembered, period of life where most of the daily discussion was how to assure the darkest tan (unaware of the real dangers of later skin cancer), and other important matters, mostly reflections on the nubile female form. Even then one knew it was an innocent, even unreal, interlude before one had to face the very real problems of life and death with those who couldn't take for granted good looks, great strength, or even health.

On Being Short
American Journal of Sports Medicine, 1999

As an obviously compassionate fourteenth birthday gift, my parents gave me a book entitled *Short Sports Heroes*. Although I had participated fully in boyhood athletics, it was becoming physiologically clear that I would never bring a tall, well-formed body to the field. The book was clearly intended to encourage me to find role models in high diving, horse racing, and other competitive sports where the emphasis was on quick reflexes and agility. I should, it was subtly suggested, emulate the feats of the diver Sammy Lee or the great jockey Eddie Arcaro.

The book probably did help redirect my energies from failed efforts at basketball or football. I became a fairly proficient swimmer. At the age of 16, in fact, despite being 5'6" and weighing 140 pounds, I secured a summer job as a lifeguard. I kept that job for the next seven years, and it partially paid my way through medical school. The reason my lifeguard career flourished was quite simple. In that era most lifeguards were "career men"; they would travel to Florida in the winter and back to Long Island in the summer. What they possessed in muscle power was rarely matched in the intellectual sphere. Some of them, sad to say, were barely able to read or write.

So, as a short lad of 16, I entered the lowest rung of the lifeguard hierarchy. I can recall how proud I was of that first lifeguard bathing suit, the whistle, and the incredible joy of pulling a drowning child from the surf. But reality soon intruded on this idyllic beach life.

On a hot July 4th, a strike was called over the very important issue of whether lifeguards had to rake seaweed from the beachfront. The lifeguards felt it embarrassing, particularly in front of their girlfriends, to undertake such a lowly job, and they went to the picket line in 95 degree temperatures on a crowded Independence Day at the Town Park. The elderly, staid Commissioner tried to reason with the senior lifeguards but was greeted with a string of four letter words, a fairly common means of lifeguard locker room communication. The Commissioner promptly ejected the lifeguard leaders and vowed that the strike could continue all summer, "through Labor Day if need be."

Maybe the impending idea of a summer off the lifeguard stands, a perch from which they could command (and be admired), made the leaders desperate enough to turn to their youngest, shortest, but possibly most talkative, new colleague. I was asked to intervene and try to convince the Commissioner that these muscular men meant no harm by their earthy expressions, and that their cause was just. After a few hours, the Commissioner agreed with my logic, but insisted that, henceforth he would deal only with me.

I became the Chief Lifeguard, a position I held for the next seven years. For me, summers became a wondrous time, with daily swimming and the added, almost unique, experience of being administrator over eighty-five decent, but trouble-prone, musclemen. Many of the lessons learned on the beach have helped me in the practice of medicine – how to understand the dreams and desires of an utterly different group of men, and how to make those who were uneducated feel part of a team. These are lessons we all must use daily in hospital work today. I've stayed in touch with a number of the lifeguards and every five years they have a reunion that allows me, now slightly below 5' 6" (as age shrinks me ever closer to Eddie Arcaro's size), to stand with the other retired Chiefs and the assembled aging beach athletes who still dream of their glory days in sun, sand, and waves.

As I fondly remember my parents' gift of love, a book for a boy of 14 trying to find the right athletic niche, encouraged to be a "short sports hero," I realize how fortunate I was to find that summer job in which I had great fun, learned a lot, and, by settling the great "seaweed strike," even contributed to preserving the dignity of lifeguards.

Suffering and Pain
Catholic Near East Magazine, 1984

A physician's view of suffering is tempered by constant exposure to pain. While philosophers and theologians may ponder the societal value of suffering, the medical doctor must deal daily with the evils of uncontrolled pain, and help resolve in the individual patient the apparent tension between theological theory and clinical reality.

The control of pain is the fundamental mandate of medicine. The incredibly rich history of medicine – possibly the noblest record of human activity – is the tale of an endless search for the means to free patients from the destructive impact of pain. One of the foundations of modern medicine was the discovery of anesthesia in the nineteenth century. Only then could prolonged surgery be performed and complicated childbirth, for example, be managed with care. Until that time pain was always the limiting factor; panic a predictable response; shock or death the inevitable result.

Medicine has evolved as both a science and an art. The ability to measure observations, to objectively record impressions, to devise specific techniques that allow comparisons over time – these are the essential methods of the science of medicine. One can, for example, determine the extent of damage to a heart muscle through the tracing of an electrocardiogram and measure the amount of morphine required to eradicate the sensation of pain. But in dealing with pain, the science of medicine does not have the tools to measure a victim's concerns, or fears, or suffering.

Each patient brings to his or her illness a certain cultural and personal influence. It is through an understanding of the mystery of the patient's uniqueness that the good physician practices the art of medicine. This elusive quality of medicine, a most subtle experience, permits the physician to share in the patient's suffering while simultaneously alleviating pain.

The Archbishop of New York, Terence Cardinal Cooke, referred to his last few months on earth as a "grace-filled time of my life." It was a time when the world watched a saintly man approach death while celebrating life in a series of memorable messages. It was also a time of agonizing pain distilled into edifying suffering. For this physician, it was a time when the science and the art of medicine coalesced.

Pain was an evil whose wince and grimace and cry could not be made romantic by any rhetoric; it had to be conquered so that the Cardinal could continue the life he loved and prepare, through prayer and suffering, for the eternal reward he sought. Drugs had to be constantly titrated so that pain could be tolerated without sacrificing the mental clarity so necessary for his final contributions. The patient who experiences that creative tension between suffering and pain must be sustained by medical craft and clinical skills. Thus, the perspective of the physician is indispensable to even the spiritual assessment of this complex and universal experience.

A Medical Student's Impressions of India
Extract from the New York State Journal of Medicine, 1960

These are introductory paragraphs from my first article in a medical journal that held, in retrospect, seeds for a future career in tropical medicine and international health.

The crowd had gathered slowly, and sheltering themselves from the 105 degree heat, the natives waited in the shade of mango trees. By noon, there were a few hundred people dressed in saris, dhotis, or nothing at all. From habit they grouped themselves so that all the lepers were under one tree, those with scabies were under another, and those with malnutrition and new complaints were under a third. They came, as they come each week, with their two annas (one penny), their tin cans, ragged clothes, hope, and trust. For this was the day the bus from the central hospital in south India arrived at its roadside clinics. Within an hour and a half, the doctors had come and gone, and the villagers were alone again for another week. Many areas do not have a rural health program which is even this extensive. Yet this is where three hundred odd million people live, dream, and die. Often this is considered the fulcrum between Eastern and Western ideologies. This is the soil of the future. This is India today.

By a very fortunate set of circumstances, a grant was made available so that I might spend a summer before graduating from medical school traveling around the world. Through the honesty and frankness of the people of the nations I visited, I had the privilege of observing first-hand the conditions in which one half of the world's population exists.

There were many obvious benefits from the trip. For me, it was a broadening experience socially, culturally, and medically.

A section of the world unfolded with a heritage far older than our Western one, with problems that are but history in the United States, and with struggles we have never known. One quickly loses the idea that our system, be it in medicine or any other field, is the only one, or even that it is the best one for situations so foreign to those in America.

It Ain't Necessarily So
2003

I am grateful for the opportunity to honor the memory of a great surgeon and admired colleague who made a major contribution to Lenox Hill Hospital. Since I can contribute nothing to surgical knowledge, I was initially puzzled as to what should be the topic of this talk. As happens so often in life – or at least it has been true in my life – the solution came from a most unexpected source. I was listening to the George Gershwin opera, *Porgy and Bess*, and the classic song, *It Ain't Necessarily So,* got me thinking.

I hope to develop a cohesive lecture for you, one that begins a long time ago, when everything seemed so easy and direct; it then moves on to philosophic reflections and some detailed consideration of two tropical infections; the talk then goes forward four decades, citing two other infections once considered "tropical" but now known as important bioterrorist agents; and ends with further reflections on our profession, security, and life.

I had gone to medical school and learned the formulas, memorizing the signs and symptoms of diseases, the useful acronyms, the differential diagnoses, the optimal therapies, and even the exact doses. My father and brothers were doctors, and I looked forward to a traditional career in the practice of medicine.

But it wasn't to be. I was fortunate – and that's where the trouble started – to travel widely at an early stage of my career. One quickly, and recurrently, came to realize that "it ain't necessarily so." All those lessons you learn in the Bible, according to the song, ain't necessarily so. And the same, at least in my experience, has been true, in a career in tropical medicine.

The absolute teachings from my medical school days were, and are, the foundation of my professional life. But too many dogmatic teachings simply didn't stand up to the new realities I faced; what professors taught as optimal solutions proved to be "ain't necessarily so."

In fact, in the tropics, one had to adapt in order to survive. One developed a healthy skepticism, a respectful questioning, probing, experimental approach; this is the philosophic basis for all research. I shall offer two examples in my tropical medicine career, where new observations fundamentally changed the understanding and management of two major infections. The teachings of the classic texts ain't necessarily so, at least forever.

The filarial infections hold an honored place in the history of tropical medicine. When Patrick Manson, in 1877, in Amoy, China, demonstrated that *Aedes* mosquitoes transmitted filaria from man to man, this was the first time that arthropod vectors were identified as an essential element in the life cycle of a disease. The filarial infections cause widespread, horrible elephantiasis of legs, scrota, and breasts and can damage the renal system resulting in patients urinating milky lymph fluid, or chyluria. These are widespread infections around the globe. Manson's discovery of insect transmission predates by twenty years the work of Ronald Ross on the role of *Anopheles* mosquitoes in malaria. His early definition of the life cycle of the different forms of filariases and their clinical severity explains why these diseases were so well studied, and why their pathology and therapy were presented so unequivocally to a young student beginning tropical medicine in London in the early 1960s.

As often happens in research, an accidental exposure to a new technique stimulated my interest in this ancient scourge. I attended a lecture by an English urologist who had developed a method of illuminating lymphatic structures in patients with testicular carcinoma. I went to my Professor at the London School of Tropical Medicine and asked whether I might try this technique in patients with filariasis. The good Professor pointed out, quite validly, that I was not licensed to practice medicine in England, but then graciously noted that he would not be in the hospital on Saturdays. With a dear, now deceased, friend we built a primitive machine to inject an oily contrast material into the lymphatics of ten filarial patients at the Hospital for Tropical Diseases. Those x-ray pictures gave the very first images of lymphatic damage in living patients with elephantiasis and chyluria; the radiographic images simply did not support the standard therapies.

We had been taught to cut away damaged, swollen tissue on elephantoid limbs and cover the areas with skin grafts; to strip perinephric lymphatics in patients with filarial chyluria. The lymphangiographic images proved this was folly; the primary problem in filariasis was fibrosis around dead worms in regional lymph nodes. Stripping away collateral lymphatic beds would only make things worse. I went on to do further lymphangiographic studies for several years at the Naval Medical Research Unit in Egypt and to write numerous articles and chapters on our findings. All accepted teachings just ain't necessarily so. Today, based in large part on understandings permitted through lymphangiograms, the management of filarial patients is utterly different from that taught to this respectful but curious student some forty years ago.

My second tropical medicine example that it all "ain't necessarily so" is again based on some observation that simply didn't fit the classic textbook descriptions we had been taught. The leishmaniases are a group of illnesses that, depending on the species, can affect the skin or cause a severe, systemic infection. Even in the 1960s, leishmania species could be well differentiated by their reservoirs, vectors, and behavior on culture media; now they can be even more precisely differentiated by isoenzyme electrophoresis, reactivity with monoclonal antibodies and by kinetoplast DNA. Forty years ago, the different species were considered as students we had to memorize maps that delineated the endemic zones for visceral disease (kala-azar), for cutaneous, and for mucocutaneous leishmaniasis.

I was assigned to investigate a large outbreak of fulminant kala-azar in the southern Sudan. This highly fatal disease causes significant liver, spleen, bone marrow, and reticuloendothelial damage. There were no reports of cutaneous leishmaniasis in this area. But once again, this proved to be not necessarily so. I began to observe skin lesions in some of the expatriate doctors and nurses. At first, I failed to make any connection. But they were indolent sores and did not respond to antibiotic therapy. Aspiration smears showed typical Leishman-Donovan bodies and cultures documented that these organisms were identical with those isolated from our kala-azar cases. But that kala-azar species was not—according to all the textbooks of the time—supposed to cause skin lesions; and in the area there were no appropriate vectors or reservoirs for cutaneous leishmanial transmission.

At the time, I speculated that distinct strains need not necessarily produce identical disease in different hosts. What if a person was well nourished, and rested, or taking some unrelated prophylactic medication? Couldn't that influence the clinical manifestation? What is accepted as dogma just ain't so. It took many years, and dozens of articles and presentations, before tropical medicine could embrace, as a fundamental, basic concept, that host and parasite live in a balance and that signs and symptoms of a single disease vary widely. This is why infants and the frail, malnourished elderly die in refugee camps and why those of us, healthy expatriates who might acquire the same disease, survive.

I will conclude with some philosophic reflections about current challenges. All of us in medicine know that ours is a profession built on traditions—noble, ancient principles and values—that guide our everyday practices. But traditions are not meant to be merely preserved and venerated; they should not be barriers to new thoughts. Our traditions allow—in fact, demand—that we question, that we investigate, try to push the limits, expand the envelope. Each medical career is different, influenced by unexpected fates and fortunes. Residents and fellows undergoing long and rigorous training might innocently believe that their professional paths will be almost predictable. Once again, I would suggest it ain't necessarily so. And once again, I would like to tell a story, one that has evolved from experiences in tropical medicine to the challenges of counterterrorism. They are not unrelated fields, as I shall try to explain.

During my years in Africa and the Middle East, I saw hundreds of patients with anthrax. There was an abattoir next door to our fever hospital and research center. Anthrax was a common occupational hazard for the tanners. I also cared for many smallpox patients in India and Somalia. Smallpox, one of the most terribly deforming and often fatal diseases, was considered eradicated more than thirty years ago and was largely forgotten, except by those who had known its devastation, and by a new generation who were supposed to carefully retain samples of live virus in two laboratories, one in the United States and one in the Soviet Union. Unfortunately, the planned security for the dangerous stockpiles proved woefully inadequate. The Russian lab disintegrated with the collapse of the Soviet Union and stores of smallpox cannot be found.

When anthrax appeared in New York in 2001, and the threat of smallpox as a deadly biological weapon was appreciated, I was asked by the New York Police Department to serve as Chief Medical Advisor for Counterterrorism. Names change, but the cycle of service continues. Two "tropical" infections had become part of our nation's life.

I have tried, in honor of a great surgeon, his family and friends, to tell a story with a number of related themes. My tale celebrates the diverse challenges we face along our careers, and it asks, particularly the young members of our profession, to listen and learn from the lessons of your mentors, but always keep an open and questioning mind. It is only by investigating your educated hunches and pursuing the puzzling aspects of our discipline, that you will push to the frontiers where questions and dreams rub, sometimes roughly, sometimes with stimulation, against reality. There, in the midst of chaos and apparent disaster, one might find, as I have been so fortunate to experience, the thrill of discovery and come to realize, as Gabriel Garcia Marquez once wrote, and as I have tried to show from Calcutta to Somalia and the Sudan to New York, *that love can flourish even in times of cholera.*

Romance and Reality in Humanitarian Action
2013

I modified this talk for university, professional and lay audiences from Massachusetts to Montana, and overseas; the basic message—that there are flowers among the weeds in life—was the same, while examples were often local and, hopefully, appropriate. This talk was delivered in the Lyford Cay Club in the Bahamas.

In the Prologue to his *Autobiography*, the Nobel Laureate,

Bertrand Russell, captured, at age 90, motivations I have identified with since my twenties. Russell wrote:

Three passions, simple but overwhelmingly strong, have governed my life: the longing for love, the search for knowledge, and unbearable pity for the suffering of mankind. These passions, like great winds, have blown me hither and thither, in a wayward course, over a great ocean of anguish, reaching to the very verge of despair. Love and knowledge, so far as they were possible, led me upward towards the heavens. But always pity brought me back to earth. Echoes of cries of pain reverberate in my heart. Children in famine, victims tortured by oppressors, helpless old people a burden to their sons, and the whole world of loneliness, poverty, and pain make a mockery of what human life should be. I long to alleviate this evil, but I cannot, and I too suffer.

C.P Snow noted in *Science and Government* that, "No one I have read has found the right answers. Very few have asked the right questions. The best I can do is tell a story." So tonight I will offer you a few connected, very personal, observations drawn from a life-long journey to many troubled parts of the world, and then leave ample time to hear your views and exchange ideas in the lovely ambiance of Lyford Cay. My title for tonight's talk should probably have been reversed for appreciating the *reality* of life is essential in discovering true *romance*.

There are definite, harsh *realities* in humanitarian fieldwork, and no amount of diplomatic sophistry can dehumanize the horrors of war and the waste of innocent lives. They are not dull statistics, but real people, who suffer and die in such situations. In the sad settings of refugee camps, mothers and children are the disposable refuse of global insecurity; becoming a child soldier or a sex slave are terribly realistic options for innocent youngsters.

But it is at times of great calamity and suffering – in humanitarian crises – where the developed and developing worlds most intimately interact, and therein lies the challenge. These occasions, if mismanaged, cause further divisions in an ever-more polarized world between the "haves" and the "have-nots." But, if handled correctly, with forethought and planning, with sensitivity and clinical efficiency, then something profoundly good may emerge. There may be no more important arena in which universally accepted standards needed to be urgently applied than in the repetitive humanitarian crises that shame our so-called civilization.

In conflict zones, a physician deals not only with the physical effects of trauma but also with the dark and tangled roots of hatred, and the incipient revenge that blossoms in such unrelenting misery. Yet with patience, and respect for others' human dignity, by balancing passion and compassion, by practicing civility and trying to understand the bases for hostility in those we assist, one can learn many lessons – particularly from the dispossessed and oppressed – and develop a special approach to life. Titles rarely matter very much in such situations. Friendships and traditions do. They maintain our spirits, especially during difficult times, and produce rich memories, as well as the necessary resolution to carry on very hard work.

One quickly becomes aware that there are no simple answers to the multiple problems that face victims of natural and man-made disasters, and that solutions, when they can be constructed, draw on many disciplines. When I first began working in humanitarian crises more than 50 years ago, we had to devise definitions to describe our goals and actions. Words, simple phonetic sounds, had to be created to characterize the levels of chaos that follow disasters, and distinguish distinct phases of response. Such crises – almost always with political and military components, and involving large numbers of people – have been the primary area of my work and teaching.

After my wife died almost nine years ago I recall sitting up at night making multiple, maybe silly, lists – one documented that I had worked at that time in 65 countries, mostly in refugee camps, in conflict and post-conflict situations, or after natural or man-made disasters. Disaster management is an evolving science, embracing every stage from prevention and preparedness, through rapid assessment and cluster assignments, all the way to reconstruction and development.

When I was young, and very innocent, I thought I was inordinately important as a medical doctor in a refugee camp. It didn't take very long to look around and realize, with growing humility, that those in charge of water or food or shelter or security or sanitation or education were indispensible partners.

It also didn't take long to realize that no one could accomplish very much working alone. One of the main obstacles that had to be overcome, if there was to be any progress in restoring a semblance of stability for those who had lost everything, were our own restrictive professional barriers.

Rigid definitions of duty cripple programs in the field. There is that inevitable time when, at least in my experience, one must move beyond the traditional confines of any discipline. There had been no courses—except possibly in philosophy, or anthropology, or comparative literature—that prepared me for the almost bizarre demands one faces in establishing and managing camps for tens, and hundreds of thousands of frightened, ill and endangered people, the vast majority being extremely vulnerable women and children. Three examples demonstrate different challenges that forced the expansion of my traditional role as a physician.

1. Early in my career I found myself in southern Sudan responsible not only for health concerns, but also for providing other basic human services, including security. It certainly was of little help to a young girl to tell her that her malaria was cured if she was raped every time she went foraging for firewood.

2. In 1972 an earthquake destroyed Managua, Nicaragua. I served as Chief Medical Adviser, sharing a tent with the then President. There I learned how politics and corruption can pollute so-called relief missions. A significant percentage of the international aid was openly looted by the President's cronies, and donors did not even complain for "diplomatic" reasons. One sadly realized the limitations of altruism in the face of evil.

3. Retraining and resettling large numbers of refugees was essential in Somalia after the Sahel drought caused a mass migration across Africa. I was directing camps with almost a million refugees. The only outlet was the Indian Ocean. Trying to teach nomads to abandon an age-old dependency on camels and cattle to seek survival as fisherman was an interesting exercise for an evolving tropicalist. The experiment worked, at least for a while.

There were also almost obvious diplomatic possibilities in our public health work, that could – and needed to be – exploited. Medicine offered an almost ideal platform for preventive diplomacy. For example, in the early 1960s, in the midst of a raging civil war in southern Sudan, we were able to establish what were called "corridors of tranquility," or "immunization breaks." These were de facto ceasefire zones, and eventually became temporary bridges to cooperation and a transient "peace." That "peace" didn't last, but those "corridors" are still recalled fondly by those who must now continue the search for common ground in the blood soaked sands of Darfur and South Sudan.

Managing complex humanitarian emergencies, particularly in the midst of conflicts and disasters, is not a field for amateurs. Good intentions are a common, but tragically inadequate, substitute for well-planned, carefully coordinated and implemented operations that, like a good sentence, must have a beginning, a middle, and an end. Compassion and charity are only elements in humanitarian assistance programs; alone they are self-indulgent emotions that, for a short time, may satisfy the donor but will always fail to help victims in desperate straits.

"Humanitarian crises" are rarely the result of just a failure of the humanitarian system. Solutions, therefore, will not be found by merely addressing unmet humanitarian needs. Slowly, but steadily, such philosophic observation led me, more and more, deeply into the uncharted seas that influence complex humanitarian crises. Some factors – medical, demographic, epidemiologic, logistical – are easily measured, and an effective response can usually be formulated. Yet it is those less definable, more subjective forces that so often determine the course of events. As in human relations, it is usually the subtle, but utterly essential, influences of natural empathy and understanding; a respect for the diversity of humanity; an appreciation of others' values and customs; a willingness to cooperate, and share; the courage to give, and to love, that most often provide the critical defining balance between success and failure.

Professionals in humanitarian assistance must approach those in pain in a nonjudgmental manner. They learn to leave behind their pride, and their preconceptions, and to sublimate their own interests and agendas in an act of solidarity with refugees and displaced persons who need their help. One learns to tread softly, to offer change with great care. One quickly finds that existing customs and practice in any community, even in the chaos of a refugee camp, must not be altered without consultation and deliberation. The ways of a people, sometimes quite incomprehensible to one trained in a Western scientific system, are ultimately that group's own precious heritage and protection. Attempts to introduce new methods, and replace time-worn approaches can be devastating, especially in times of crises, when their society is extremely vulnerable and utterly dependent on strangers for the essentials of life.

When I first began working in complex humanitarian crises there were no accepted standards or training programs; in fact, there wasn't even, as I already noted, a common vocabulary. What was desperately needed was the creation of a new profession, one that could embrace the many areas of expertise required to provide an overall response. This is where academia had to enter the picture. We began, several decades ago, to develop new, practical, university level programs geared to the unique needs of international aid workers. Through Fordham University's Institute of International Humanitarian Affairs one can now take an undergraduate Major, or a postgraduate Masters degree in this field. In training experienced humanitarian workers we now have over 2000 graduates from 133 nations. Whatever our differences in cultural background, or material fortune, we all share a common destiny, and working to realize that forges close bonds that ultimately tie us together.

Our best-known program, the International Diploma in Humanitarian Assistance (IDHA), is a month-long, 12 hours per day, residential course that simulates the multiple challenges faced in complex humanitarian crises. The average IDHA candidate is 38 years of age, has had 5 years of field experience, and represents all the disciplines required for an effective emergency relief response. On most IDHA courses we have physicians, nurses, military, academics and logistics experts; we have had judges from the International Criminal Court in The Hague as well as missionaries. Our graduates work in almost every U.N. agency, major international NGO and, most importantly, in local government and volunteer relief groups around the world.

So much for *reality*; I now turn to *romance*. My wife used to say that I was the only person she knew who could come home after three months in a Somali refugee camp and keep her awake all night describing, in great detail, how beautiful it was. Yes, there were incredible scenes of sadness and evil, but there were also exquisite sunrises and sunsets in the desert; the unexpected sound of children laughing; and the incredible strength of mothers and grandmothers coping in a daily struggle to survive. So that is my second, and equally important, theme – the beauty and *romance* of life. Much depends on how the mind's eye sees, and interprets, the fields in which we work.

Over fifty years ago I arrived in Calcutta, and fell in love with a way of life. I find romance in settings that others might – quite legitimately – see only as dirty, broken down wastelands. Surely those negatives existed in Calcutta. But amidst the fetid stenches of Indian urban decay, I mainly recall the strong aroma of exotic spices. I close my eyes but usually see saffron robes rather than soiled rags. I hear music in the cacophonous sounds of the slums, and in the long silence of a city drenched in the humid heat that comes with monsoon rains.

Over the next four months I attended, every morning, clinical rounds at the All India Institute of Tropical Medicine; but being young and indefatigable, I also spent every afternoon helping to tend the dying in a gutter with a then unknown Albanian nun the world now remembers as Mother Theresa. I was immersed in a wonder-filled, strange culture, and faced utterly new challenges and, just as importantly, new opportunities.

One of the most important lessons of India that has remained with me for life, and helped determine what I have tried to do, and how, was the realization that one must stay calm and focused in the midst of chaos in order to help others. There was no time for self-indulgent, personal concerns. The petty needs that so often dominate our lives distract us from getting critical tasks accomplished. One quickly learned, with embarrassment, that our own individual cares simply didn't matter much in the face of what others were suffering everyday, all day, in the disaster that life offered them.

Since then, during a very full, joyous career – if that is an appropriate definition for a journey where there were few guideposts along the way – I've worked all over the world, mostly in refugee camps and war zones. I saw plenty of tragedy during those travels, and there are scenes seared into my soul – the appalling waste of life, and of human dignity; pain that I was often helpless to relieve; the stares of starving children, and the dying gasps of too many mothers in childbirth. Yet, I always realized how privileged I was to serve, to share, and even begin to identify with those caught in the cross fires of conflicts not of their making. A spiritual solidarity develops in just being with them. They were my brothers and sisters.

In the most sordid situations I have, often with amazement, always with admiration, seen the indomitable courage and resiliency of the downtrodden, those who seem to have been totally overwhelmed, but then, like the Phoenix, rise again from the ashes. I have always returned – but, in some important ways, I never returned – from refugee camps grateful to be allowed to participate in their valiant efforts.

Relief work in the developing world is often frustrating, and progress can be very slow indeed. Accomplishments are rarely grandiose. I recall asking a former professor, one of the great academic mentors in my life, what he thought he had accomplished after 5 years trying – and ultimately failing – to establish a medical school in the southern Sudan. "What have you really done?" I asked. After a few minutes, he responded, "I think the drain in front of the clinic works."

I have helped, even healed, many desperate victims in humanitarian crises, and, in turn, they helped, healed, instructed and changed me. I have been the recipient of their kindnesses – they who had so little gave their meager supplies to me, and, on more than one occasion, offered to protect me with their lives, for that is the obligation of a host in the remote Islamic lands that were, for years, my home. I learned much about the values of clan loyalty and family love around campfires in the deserts of Somalia and Sudan, from elders who were guided by values as noble as our Judeo-Christian traditions. My outlook, and my message for you, are greatly influenced by them.

I have been caught behind the lines in armed conflicts, and seen senseless slaughter from Beirut to Managua, and all across the scarred landscape of modern Africa. Somehow in the twisted wreckage of war, and in the squalor of refugee camps, the incredible beauty of humanity prevailed for me, as it does for most of those privileged to work in humanitarian assistance. It is that perspective that sustains us on what otherwise might seem like an endless trip through hell on earth.

Being dog-dirty and exhausted was a very small price to pay for knowing one could slowly bring order out of confusion, hope out of despair, determination out of fear. These were the incalculable, almost indescribable, rewards. It takes time to refocus the romance of youth into reflective, lasting programs in humanitarian crises, to change the passion of love into healing projects. One learned from errors and failures, and then struggled ahead, with more hard work. As Samuel Beckett once wrote, we must "Try again. Fail again. Fail better."

My wife, Kate, came with me to many troubled areas around the world; she was not a physician or a health worker, but she was my indispensable partner, sharing in all the routine, basic chores that are part of everyday humanitarian work. She was my moral compass. It would certainly have been easier—and safer—to reap the rewards assured by a predictable medical practice at home. But that was not what fate offered us. We discovered a new world—and ourselves—in the midst of revolutions; several of them were planned in our living room. We were able to share in the dreams and aspirations of men and women in the Third World who were fighting for freedom, for equality, for basic human rights, and often for their very survival.

In such situations, silence and isolation are simply not viable options. In this era of instant communications, basic moral values make it impossible for any of us to hide from massive sufferings. We just are not free to stay in some blissful state of denial, to think that expressions of concern, or endless discussions, will suffice. Ultimately, each of us must find our own way, hone our own tools, as we continue the journey of life—a trek where I hope you too will find beauty and companionship and joy, where the initial impression may seem like only blood and sweat and tears.

That at least has been my experience. Maybe my tales will broaden your horizons, and even help you in love, for that is what drives us onwards. Love, ultimately, is all that matters. It is the substance and cement that binds us together. It is important to see both the *romance* and the *reality* in life, and to never, ever, allow yourself to be fenced in by futile obsessions with self-security or fear or despair.

Most of you already know from life's experiences that there is often more beauty and understanding, consideration and self-growth to be found on harsh and difficult frontiers than in the refined protected environments of the establishment. Verities do not change with time or with continents; they are the same in Mogadishu or Managua or Lyford Cay.

I thank you for the privilege of being with you – and hope that we may all continue to find flowers hidden amidst the weeds of life.

This book began with reflections written after leading a Pontifical Mission to a war zone in Lebanon in late spring of 1982, and it ends with personal memories of a critical time in the life of Pope John Paul II. This photo captures, I believe, the trust and warmth that often develops in a physician-patient relationship. I was departing for the United States after meeting the Holy Father in the papal summer residence at Castel Gandolfo, in the cool hills outside Rome. I briefed him on a rather hazardous but successful journey of peace in his name in Lebanon. Our entourage was once caught in a fierce crossfire between Israeli and Palestinian forces. Later that day our car was commandeered by a fringe element of the

PLO, *the* Murabitun. *Masked men with AK-47s bundled a good monsignor and myself into the back seat and drove us up a dead end road. We were ordered to get out with our hands above our heads, while they tried, quite in vain, to give reassurance that they really didn't want to hurt us. They explained that they merely wanted to siphon the gas from our car, and we then would be free to coast down hill to the relative safety of the bombed out center of town. We found our way home in an ambulance.*

To Bear Witness
America, 2005 / FIDES, The Vatican, 2005

Shortly after completing emergency abdominal surgery on Pope John Paul II, following an assassination attempt in May 1981, his Vatican and hospital medical team asked six international specialists to come to Rome and serve as consultants. Two of those invited were from the United States, the senior Professor of Surgery at Harvard, and myself. The consultants met with the Italian doctors, examined the patient, reviewed the hospital records, and issued appropriate bulletins. Newspaper and television coverage made our participation part of the public record.

While most of the other consultants believed it appropriate to provide follow-up interviews, I have always felt this should be done only if specifically requested by the patient and, therefore, declined all requests. The Pope, and his then Secretary of State, Cardinal Casaroli, wrote to me of their appreciation for my help and discretion.

After his discharge to the Vatican, the Pope developed recurrent fevers and had to be readmitted to the Gemelli hospital. I was asked to return to Rome, this time alone, and remained there for over a month assisting in his care. Although I shall not provide medical details of this period, I am persuaded by some who knew the Holy Father well that it would be fitting, now that he has died, to record this remarkable man's reactions to a life-threatening and, I believe, life-changing crisis.

Many of the qualities and strengths of his personality that have so impressed the world were distilled to a very fine point in that hospital room. Even in his weakened state, he was clearly a patient intent on living; he had utter confidence that he would survive and was determined to recover as quickly as possible. He was a cooperative and obedient patient, willing to experience intrusive examinations without complaint. In a lifetime's practice of medicine, I cannot recall a better example of a very ill patient combining humility and inherent nobility. He had obvious respect for, and offered constant and lasting gratitude to, his doctors. His acceptance of his physically compromised condition reminded me of the daily dialogue in medicine that allows the sick to break out of their prisons of pain, and which permits health workers to grow stronger by involvement in suffering and death.

During his recuperation, when long conversations were easier and personal trust had developed, I was most impressed by his range of interests; he seemed informed on almost any topic from world events to modern American music, from Irish art and mythology to African sculpture. He would silently listen, absorbing ideas and opinions, and then cite some of these early conversations to me years later. He was intensely curious, asked provocative questions, and shared his convictions and optimism in poetic and, still to me, memorable phrases. We maintained contact over the next few decades as I travelled through Rome on my way to various humanitarian missions. I never ceased to be amazed at his thoughtfulness and kindness.

I was not involved in his medical care in recent years; but that he decided to fully express his own love of life to the very end—despite progressive frailty and obvious suffering—was no surprise to this physician. I was privileged to have served him in a critical period, and I am now able to bear unique witness to the qualities that made Pope John Paul II a remarkable influence in an often shallow and fickle world.

Sannes woods – 2003
Walking in my heavy Irish tweed coat,
with damp moss underfoot, and a pensive
look reflecting both past joys and future
worries, Kate captured, in her last photo of
me, the Celtic musing part of a personality
that had become irretrievably intertwined
with her own.
That shared foundation was essential
to all that had gone before – or would
come. The perspective that is grounded in
experiences of famine and war
and oppression, and, most importantly,
with the reality and confidence of love, are
all in this photo of a stage on a journey.

For Your 65th

You've flirted, teased
And danced with death
Baiting—taunting
Living life to the limit
Of your imagination

And what else is there?
You used this time of being
To bring joy—to help others
To stretch the limits of your
Talent and your humanity

Never caring for the dull mind—the
Darkness—the ones who live
Without light; because you can't
Foresee a life without love—without feeling

Flouting fear you reject
The inane, the uncomprehending
Those who deny
Daring them to see what few have seen

You soared and swooped
Like a bird, challenging
Everything, even the unknown
And you bring
Light to the world by your
Love of the sensual
The tactile joy of living.
By example—you are the Word.

Kathryn Cahill
Poems and Photographs, 2004

The Center for International Humanitarian Cooperation and the Institute of International Humanitarian Affairs

The Center for International Humanitarian Cooperation (CIHC) was founded in 1992 to promote healing and peace in countries shattered by natural disasters, armed conflicts, and ethnic violence. The Center employs its resources and unique personal contacts to stimulate interest in humanitarian issues and to promote innovative educational programs and training models. The CIHC has sponsored symposia, exhibits, and published numerous books and Occasional Papers, including the International Humanitarian Book Series of Fordham University Press.

The CIHC has collaborated with Fordham University to foster close links between academia and humanitarian field operations, creating an Institute of International Humanitarian Affairs (IIHA). Its flagship course is the International Diploma in Humanitarian Assistance (IDHA). The IIHA also offers a graduate Master's Degree in International Humanitarian Action (MIHA) and an undergraduate International Humanitarian Affairs major program. The IIHA also offers specialized training courses for humanitarian negotiators, international human rights lawyers, and mental health workers in war zones. Short (one–to two-week) courses in forced migration, humanitarian law, mental health in complex emergencies, and civil military cooperation, among others, are presented in countries around the world. In the past few academic years, courses were offered in seventeen countries across five continents. For more information, visit www.fordham.edu/iiha.

The Directors of the CIHC serve as the Advisory Board of the IIHA. The President of the CIHC is the University Professor and Director of the Institute; the CIHC Humanitarian Programs Director is Visiting Professor at the IIHA; other CIHC Directors are Diplomats in Residence at Fordham University.

Directors
Kevin M. Cahill, M.D. — President
David Owen — Secretary
Francis Deng
Boutros Boutros-Ghali
Richard Goldstone
Helen Hamlyn
Peter Hansen
Nassir Abdulaziz al-Nasser
Eoin O'Brien, M.D.
Joseph A. O'Hare, S.J.
Peter Tarnoff
Larry Hollingworth — Humanitarian Program Director
Brendan Cahill — Executive Director, IIHA

IIHA Book Series

The International Humanitarian Affairs book series, edited by Kevin M. Cahill, M.D., is devoted to improving the effectiveness of humanitarian relief programs. With contributions by leading professionals, the books are practical guides to responding to the many different effects of civil strife, natural disasters, epidemics, and other crises. Most books are available online at www.fordhampress.com. Books marked with an asterisk are available in French translation from Robert Laffont of Paris.

Preventive Diplomacy: Stopping Wars Before They Start, 2000*
Basics of International Humanitarian Missions, 2003*
Emergency Relief Operations, 2003*
Traditions, Values, and Humanitarian Action, 2003*
Human Security for All: A Tribute to Sergio Vieira de Mello, 2004
Technology for Humanitarian Action, 2004
To Bear Witness: A Journey of Healing and Solidarity, 2005*
Tropical Medicine: A Clinical Text, 7th edition, 2006
The Pulse of Humanitarian Assistance, 2007
Even in Chaos: Education in Times of Emergency, 2010
Sudan at the Brink: F. D. Deng, 2010, with Foreword by Kevin M. Cahill, M.D.*
Tropical Medicine: A Clinical Text, 8th edition (Jubilee Edition), 2011*
More with Less: Disasters in an Era of Diminishing Resources, 2012
History and Hope: The International Humanitarian Reader, 2013

IIHA Occasional Papers

Kevin M. Cahill, M.D., Abdulrahim Abby Farah, Abdirazak
Haji Hussein, and David Shinn,
The Future of Somalia: Stateless and Tragic, 2004
Mark Malloch Brown,
International Diploma in Humanitarian Assistance, 2006
Francis Deng,
Sudan: From Genocidal Wars to Frontiers of Peace and Unity, 2006
Kevin M. Cahill, M.D.,
The University and Humanitarian Action, 2008
Kevin M. Cahill, M.D.,
Romance and Reality in Humanitarian Action, 2008
Kevin M. Cahill, M.D.,
Gaza—Destruction and Hope, 2009
Daithi O'Ceallaigh,
The Tale Towards a Treaty—A Ban on Cluster Munition, 2010